THE COCKTAIL SHAKER

THE *Tanqueray* GUIDE

PHILIP WILSON PUBLISHERS

THE
COCKTAIL
SHAKER

by Simon Khachadourian

THE *Tanqueray* GUIDE

PHILIP WILSON PUBLISHERS

First published in 2000 by
Philip Wilson Publishers Ltd
143–149 Great Portland Street
London W1N 5FB

Distributed in the USA and Canada by
Antique Collectors' Club
91 Market Street Industrial Park
Wappingers' Falls
New York 12590

ISBN 0 85667 520 2

New photography by Adrian Brown and Alf Barnes

Recipes by Angus Winchester

Designed by Keith Watson

Edited by Patricia Bascom

Printed and bound in Italy by
Società Editoriale Lloyd, Srl, Trieste

CONTENTS

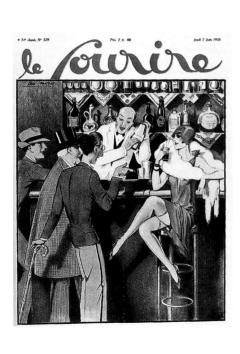

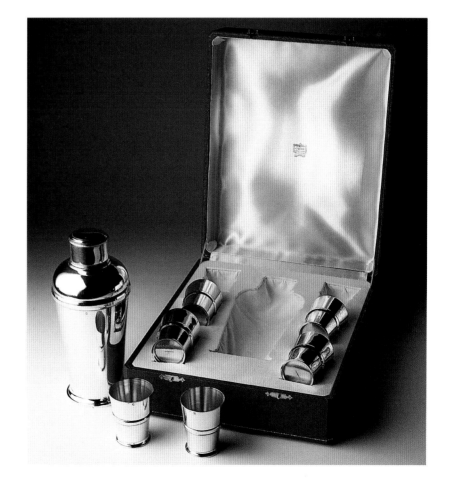

For Theadora

AUTHOR'S ACKNOWLEDGEMENTS

The creation of this book would not have been possible without the friendship and custom of the many enthusiasts and collectors who have crossed Pullman's threshold in its first couple of years, and left feeling stirred, not shaken!

I also wish to thank Rupert Prior, Ann-Marie Talbot, Neil Woodcock, Anna Astin, Mark Birley, Salvatore Calabrese and Steve Visakay for their invaluable assistance and inspiration.

Credit is also due to Adrian Brown and Alf Barnes, who are to the camera what Harry Craddock was to the cocktail shaker. I am especially honoured that Jane Bown, *grande dame* of portrait photography, agreed to include me amongst her subjects (along with Noel Coward, David Niven, Richard Burton and Mick Jagger!).

I am especially indebted to my wife Eleanor and my children, Nathalie and George, for their enthusiasm, encouragement and undiminishing sense of humour.

Simon Khachadourian
London, June 2000

FOREWORD

by Nicholas Foulkes

The cocktail shaker is one of the Western World's most potent cultural symbols. It is shorthand for a kind of civilised decadence – if that is not too much of an oxymoron. As Jane Austen never said, it is a truth universally acknowledged that a man in possession of a cocktail shaker is always ready to party.

The two-piece cocktail shaker was already an important piece of the barman's equipment by the closing years of the nineteenth century. However, the golden age of the cocktail shaker was the period between the two world wars of the last century.

It was during these years that novelist Alec Waugh, elder brother of Evelyn, claimed to have invented the cocktail party, because he needed something to fill the time between tea and dinner. The Great War had changed life forever and the young and the beautiful were in search of new methods of oblivion – the alcoholic neologism of the cocktail suited them perfectly. Exotic to taste, and guaranteed to kick-start even the dowdiest of parties, the cocktail was the beverage of choice of the Jazz Age.

The rattle of ice cubes in a silver shaker wielded by an expert barman is a soothing sound. It inspired at least two great cultural legacies: the verse of Dorothy Parker and the art of the cocktail shaker.

The artistic, social and architectural trends of the age found their expression in this most elegant and intoxicating of utensils. The great jewellers and silversmiths of the age created unique pieces for those who could afford them. And at least one serious industrial designer, Lurelle Guild, felt moved to design a cocktail serving set that looked like a skyscraper.

But while a serious matter, cocktails are not intended to be joyless and so it is appropriate that the most endearing relics of this golden age of alcohol are the novelty shakers. Some give explicit instructions on how to mix drinks, while others take the form of objects as diverse as fire extinguishers, bombs, lady's legs, lighthouses and even penguins.

However, the cocktail shaker is more than just a bartending tool; indeed, it has played its part in politics. Roosevelt's favourite cocktail shaker, decorated with a *bas relief* bamboo pattern, was as much a part of his presidency as Churchill's cigar was an emblem of his premiership. FDR and Stalin developed an understanding dubbed by one insider as the 'four martinis and let's have an agreement' approach to diplomacy.

Later, when JFK's spin-doctors wanted to give him a hep and groovy image, the Margarita was chosen as the drink to help. In all probability this recipe was mixed in the President's monogrammed silver shaker, which was later sold at an auction of the effects of the late Jackie O for a sum in excess of $20,000.

Both the electric blender and President Jimmy Carter tried to kill the cocktail shaker: the former with its push-button convenience and the latter with a plea to corporate America to wean itself off the three-martini lunch.

However, thanks to enthusiasts and trend-setters such as Simon Khachadourian, the cult of the cocktail shaker has weathered the onslaught of both technology and political correctness and survived into the twenty-first century.

Of ice and men: cocktail experts taste new recipes at Dorland Hall, London. At the turn of the century, cocktails in Britain had some way to go to attain the status they enjoyed across the Atlantic. Vermouth was considered by some to be 'dangerously Parisian'.

ORIGINS

'Nothing can replace a good cocktail shaker'
GUY DE WARREN: BAR-FLY

Thirsty something: the cocktail shaker is a uniquely American invention. Gin, the definitive cocktail base, is shown at its best when reserved for that most enduring example of the mixologist's art – the classic dry martini. Books, poems, plays and films provide countless references to classic cocktails and generally reflect the years of supremacy for gin-based versions.

Never mind who invented the cocktail shaker. On the whole, things like cocktail shakers do not get invented – they are developed. On the other hand, there is seldom much difficulty in deciding who first made a thing in practicable shape and proceeded to do it on a commercial scale. In the case of the cocktail shaker, this was unquestionably the Americans. The classic cocktail shaker, once a symbol of glamour and sophistication and now eminently collectable, is an original American invention. Mixed drinks have been around for a long time. The ancient Egyptians, who included alcohol in medicinal remedies, were known to disguise the taste of fermented drinks by adding herbs and spices. In 1520, Hernán Cortéz, the conqueror of Mexico, wrote in praise of a New World drink mixed with cacao, and poured from a cylindrical gold container.

The true origins of the first cocktail are much debated but references to cocktails appear as early as 1806. Again, it was in America that the identity and popularity of 'mixed drinks' which appeared on menus following the Civil War, was firmly established. G. F. Heublein of Connecticut was the first company to offer pre-mixed liquors in 1892 ('Would not such a drink put new life into the tired woman who has shopped all day? Would it not be the drink to offer to the husband when he returns home after his day's business?') For those not quite sure how to mix 'Club Cocktails', the Hartford firm offered a choice of seven bottled drinks – martini, Manhattan, Tom or Holland gin, vermouth, York or whiskey. By 1900, Heublein were directing their advertising more towards women ('Before you do another thing, James, bring me a CLUB cocktail. I'm so tired shopping, make it a Martini. I need a little tonic and it's so much better than a drug of any kind.') They confidently claimed their product was 'A better cocktail at home than is served in any Bar in the world'.

Books such as *The Bon Vivant's Companion, or How to Mix Drinks* by 'Professor' Jerry Thomas, principal bartender at the Metropolitan

Hotel, New York and the Planter's House, St Louis, a pioneer cocktail exponent, helped to spread the fashion for the mixed drink during the Victorian era. Thomas, at the height of his fame in the 'Roaring Fifties', toured Europe in 1859 with a set of sterling silver cups, standard mixing practice at the time, trailing a stream of liquid flame as he compounded his legendary Blue Blazer cocktail, a powerful concoction of burning whiskey and boiling water (for the novice, practice with cold water was recommended) and 'the greatest cold weather beverage of the day'. Cups, or tumblers, were succeeded by the standard two-piece cocktail shaker – two containers which fit one into the other, mix the ingredients and chill the drinks quickly.

The cocktail shaker is essentially a city dweller and it was a New Yorker, William Harnett, who applied for a design patent for improvements in 'Apparatus for Mixing Drinks in 1872', the earliest surviving claim recorded by the United States Patent Office to one of the most common implements of barware. The three-piece cocktail shaker, utilising a built-in strainer and air venting for ease of pouring, followed in 1884. Both two- and three-piece versions, with remarkably little change in form, are still in use today.

Inside view: waiters on parade in a London restaurant cocktail bar. Britain's first true cocktail bar is generally reckoned to have opened at the Criterion in Piccadilly, in 1910.

Martinez

2 parts TANQUERAY® gin
½ part dry vermouth
½ part maraschino
3 drops orange bitters

Shake all and strain into
chilled cocktail glass.

*Many historians attribute
the invention of the
martini to the Californian
town of Martinez, and
'Professor' Jerry Thomas,
the master mixologist who
travelled with a $4,000
solid silver bar set.*

The new Meriden Brittania Company, later the International Silver Company, to whom we shall return, featured six sizes of the standard two-piece cocktail shaker in their 1887 catalogue. One of the Crowned Heads among American bar chiefs, William Schmidt, author of *The Flowing Bowl, What and When to Drink*, published in 1892, delivered himself of the opinion: 'A drink well served is worth two that lack in preparation'. *The Bumper Book*, another popular title, followed in 1899, listing drinks and toasts and devised by the Gorham Company, the largest manufacturer of American silver in the nineteenth century.

During the century that opened in 1900, the cocktail shaker, primarily utilitarian in design – decoration, if any, was Victorian in style – became a bar-room fixture. Grand hotels in America which had observed the English habit of serving afternoon tea at five o'clock were well qualified to capitalise on the convention and later introduced the cocktail 'hour'. Many early cocktail shakers recall the gentility of nineteenth-century English teapots and the term 'teas' was still extant during the Thirties. In 1863, in London, the Englishmen

Variations on a theme: hammered pewter shakers in the form of coffee pots. Keystone-ware, c.1930, Liberty Tudric, c.1920. Liberty, who successfully retailed machine-made metalwork with the outward appearance of a hand-crafted finish, never revealed the names of their designers.

Party size: a fine sterling silver Cartier shaker, in company with a Poole Silver Company shaker, and another long-handled American version, c.1930. Early cocktail shakers frequently resembled tea or coffee pots. Songwriter Irvin Berlin predicted, 'you cannot make your shimmy shake on tea'.

'Shaken not stirred' (A): Peter, well-known barman at the Café Anglais in London between the wars, mixes a cocktail for the camera. For many, gin was the only proper base for mixed drinks.

Henry Porter and George Roberts, observed, 'For the sensation drinks which have lately travelled across the Atlantic we have no friendly feeling ... we will pass the American Bar ... and express our gratification at the slight success of which 'Pick-me-up', 'Corpse Reviver', 'Chain-Lightning' and the like, have had in this country'.

By 1908 Harrods department store was advertising two silver-plated examples of the cocktail shaker in their brochure ('for mixing American drinks'). Cartier, Tiffany and Asprey, among others, would be inspired to undertake unique and highly successful commissions in limited editions. The Hon. William 'Cocktail' Boothby, writing in his mixology manual, *The World's Drinks and How to Mix Them*, published in the same year, cautioned, 'Do not serve a frosted glass to a gentleman who wears a mustache, as the sugar adheres to that appendage and causes great inconvenience'. In 1911, the year of the fox-trot, dancing, drinking and dining were no longer regarded as separate recreations in America and the cocktail shaker, at the heart of the action in lavish new pleasure palaces like Murray's Roman

Gardens and Churchill's in New York, had entered the mainstream.

The rest, as the cliché has it, is history. Gradually, and sometimes controversially, the cocktail shaker, finding favour with the socially advanced in London, Paris, Copenhagen and elsewhere, moved from the bar into the home. The cocktail party, an innovation which made the social roundabout whirl faster, became an institution, influencing fashion, furniture and design. A cocktail party was acknowledged as a social event as much as a luncheon or dinner and the occasion was frequently found to help bridge the conversational gap. The age of the cocktail shaker had arrived.

'Shaken not stirred' (B): a London barman prepares a cocktail at Hector's Devonshire Restaurant. Barney Burke, the renowned American bartender, advised 'Shake cocktails gently; violent or prolonged shaking may seriously affect the vitality and bouquet'. Not everyone agreed with him.

The 'Original' Martini

2 parts TANQUERAY® gin
1 part chablis (or other
dry white wine)
pinch ground cinnamon

Shake all and serve as
cold as possible.

*Attributed to part-time
composer and alcohol
enthusiast,
J.P. Schwarzendorf
(1741–1816).
The first true martini?*

Where would the Martini be without the Cocktail Shaker?

Society's favourite cocktail, truly American and forever associated with a glamorous lifestyle and the silver screen, evokes a strong response among practitioners of the martini culture whenever the name is mentioned. The English author and playwright Somerset Maugham, a shrewd judge of a proper cocktail, has one of his characters reflect, 'when you come down to brass tacks there's nothing to beat a dry martini'. Everyone has a different way of preparing, savouring and eulogising the colourful cocktail. 'Martinis, oh boy!' wrote Victor Bergeron, familiarly known as 'Trader' Vic, 'more things are put out and called a martini than there are beans in all of Heinz's cans'. The Australian novelist Frank Moorhouse's advice, available for anyone unfortunate enough to be lost in the Outback was, 'stay where you are, mix a dry martini and within minutes someone will turn up and tell you you're doing it wrong'.

Made in China: raised dragon motifs form the decoration on these two silver cocktail shakers, manufactured in Shanghai c.1925. By the 1890s, the good machine-made object was not only a possibility but a fact and often preferable to the hand-made piece, representing a way of life no longer in keeping with the times.

Select company: superior sterling silver cocktail shakers from four famous names, Cartier, Tiffany, Asprey and Puiforcat, with swan cocktail stick-holder to the foreground.

French '75'

1 part TANQUERAY® gin
½ part lemon juice
fill with champagne

Shake gin and juice
and strain into
chilled coupé glass.
Add champagne and
garnish with lemon twist.

Preferred cocktail of French officers at Verdun, 1915. Named after a French artillery piece. Hits with remarkable precision.

The stylish cocktail base of gin – the name comes from the French *genévrier* (juniper berry) – was first made in the seventeenth century in Holland, then the most advanced and richest civilisation in Europe. It was the English who shortened the Dutch word *genever* to gin, and when the spirit was mixed with vermouth, from the German *vermut* (wormwood) a cocktail was created that was destined to achieve unequalled status. The winning combination, familiar to bartenders in the United States and Europe from the early 1900s and widely admired simultaneously by the highly conventional and the wildly eccentric, was the most desirable American cocktail before the First World War. It was calculated that over 120 recipes were in circulation by the end of the Twenties.

The English had increased their reputation for gin distilling with the evolution of their own, drier style, distinguished by distinctive botanical flavourings. Charles Tanqueray established a distillery in the Bloomsbury district of London, near the site of a pure water spa, at the age of twenty in 1830. There he developed his own brand of high-grade gin, carefully prepared from the finest ingredients and blended to a standard approved by the discerning customer willing to pay extra for quality. The premium **Tanqueray®** gin, with its characteristic green bottle – resembling the shape of a Victorian London fire hydrant but arguably showing the influence of shaker design – and red seal, is the leading imported gin brand in the United States and the preferred choice of connoisseurs for the gin martini cocktail. Over twenty million bottles are sold every year. The gin martini, once described as 'a genuine contribution to the happiness of mankind' and the archetype and model of what a cocktail should be, has enjoyed a reputation for greater popular prestige than any of its rivals. Long may it continue.

The cocktail crowd: devotees were inclined to drift to where the best cocktails were reputed to be served. It is still the same today. The cocktail party, variously attributed to war artist C. R. W. Nevinson, Alec Waugh, elder brother of Evelyn, Society hostess Madam Alfredo de Pena, and a bunch of American undergraduates at Oxford, was cheaper than a dinner party. 'I am prepared to believe that a dry martini impairs the palate' wrote Alec Waugh, 'but think what it does for the soul'.

S H A K E R S
G A L O R E

'The age demanded an image'
EZRA POUND. AMERICAN POET

New Era, new Cocktails, new Shakers

The British and the Americans, the least militarised nations of the developed world, were drawn into the First World War in 1914 and 1917, respectively. Victory in November 1918 brought rejoicing. It did not restore the old certainties of the Victorian and Edwardian age. An era had ended.

One certainty of the new world order was the change in the role of women. In Britain alone, 400,000 left domestic service during the hostilities and never took it up again, and 800,000 turned to engineering – once socially unacceptable and 'little better than labouring' – in the years when the divide between engineering and aesthetics was narrowing.

Women in America were long recognised as enjoying far less social restraint than their British counterparts, a characteristic first noted during the American War of Independence, when the women had carried on in the absence of men-folk; in the Civil War they had done the same again. Similarly, the Great War of 1914–18 brought about emancipation and British women came into their own. When the gin martini and the cocktail shaker ruled, the ritual of cocktail drinking would be shared by women and men on equal terms.

The national exuberance of the American people and the lead they gave in all social fashions as countries recovered a peacetime appearance is a keynote factor in the overall story of the cocktail shaker. Masterly innovations in shaker design followed during the 'long week-end' that featured in the Twenties and Thirties.

Both American and European manufacturers faced excess capacity following the Armistice as the demand for munitions dropped. Other uses had to be found for supplies of brass and copper and in Providence, Rhode Island the enterprising Gorham Company,

Pink Gin

3 parts TANQUERAY® gin
6 drops angostura bitters

Add gin and angosturas to ice-filled shaker. Shake all until the resulting liquid takes on a pinkish hue.

By-product of colonialism from the British. The Royal Navy used pink gin as a cure for digestive distress, encountered in the Tropics. Also drunk by Sir Francis Chichester on Gypsy Moth IV as he sailed solo round the World in 1966.

Shaker heights: Asprey twelve-bore bullet cartridge, English rocket shaker c.1930; a rare artillery shell shaker, one of the tallest ever produced, from Gorham c.1918; a late 1920s German bullet shaker, and a 1950s Italian rocket shaker.

High life by night: posing for the cameras upstairs at Isa Lancaster's club. The early Twenties saw the rapid growth of nightclubs in London – some highly respectable. The 'Night Light', for example, boasted two princesses and four peers on its committee.

founded in 1813 and synonymous with decorative tableware, showed that they were quickly back in the peacetime groove by offering a wartime legacy – the artillery shell cocktail shaker. One of the tallest ever produced, the base of a real shell was employed as a container for glasses and the upper section served as the shaker. Production continued until 1921.

As the new map of the globe was drawn in 1919, people so long deprived of pleasure were justly out to enjoy themselves. 'From the broad plateau of the Place de la Concorde to the pleasure slopes of Montmartre' wrote John Thomas in his memorably titled novel *Dry Martini: A Gentleman in Love*, 'bar after bar sprang up like mushrooms among the drab cafés'. The British gladly welcomed American influence in dress, music, dancing and fun. *Punch* magazine, priding itself on being a national institution, had printed many a cartoon against cocktail drinking and in Victorian clubland there had been no equivalent to a cocktail (cocktail bars, after appropriate hesitation, were introduced into such strongholds as White's and the St James's Club). A hostess in pre-1914 Britain did not, as a general rule, serve drinks before dinner, only wines or fruit cups were taken on social occasions, but as in other fields, fashion played its part in drinking patterns. As the 'Roaring Twenties' were ushered in, cocktails, once staunchly opposed by the British upper class, were progressively accepted. It is worthy of remark that cocktail parties in the Twenties were not yet popular enough to rouse the anger of the Church.

Syncopated music, denounced as 'barbarous and blatant' in 1912, was, in the contemporary phrase 'all the rage'. The 'newest jazzes and the latest rags' had to be learned without delay. It was noted, not for the first time, that a Jazz Age band could earn more in a season than the Prime Minister in the course of a whole year. The 'Jazz Age', a phrase particularly relevant to cocktail culture, is attributed to the American writer F. Scott Fitzgerald, from his collection of short stories *Tales of the Jazz Age*. Early financial success enabled Fitzgerald and his wife Zelda to lead the kind of boisterous existence the title suggests. The *Daily Mail*, reporting on 'This Jazz Age' said 'People are dancing as they have never danced before, in a happy rebound from the austerities of war.' There were plenty of Americans about to show them how these dance steps should be properly performed. Just when America was having the time of its life, enjoying a massive post-war bender, the government administered a shock to the nation's system. At midnight on 16 January 1920, a legal ban on the manufacture, sale or transportation of intoxicating liquors was enforced. Everything suddenly came to a standstill. The Prohibition era had begun.

Prohibitionists believed drinking threatened, among other things, the integrity of the family, and law and order. Temperance societies had been set up and the members of the Anti-Saloon League of America (ASL), who had been 'making a nuisance of themselves since 1898' to quote one commentator, mapped out a plan for effective political support. The majority of American citizens had accepted temporary Prohibition as a necessary measure in the circumstances of the First World War. Constitutional amendment followed in 1919 and Andrew Volstead, a dedicated Prohibitionist, introduced the Act to Congress. It is not without interest that Warren G. Harding, who guided the Eighteenth Amendment through the Senate, and who was to win the Presidency in 1920, was himself an enthusiastic drinker.

The arrival of Prohibition had not been unattended by trouble, boosting the fortunes of 'bootleggers' and racketeers. 'Bootlegging', the American frontier practice of smuggling liquor in boot tops, presented a promising business opportunity for organised crime, especially in Chicago, called 'Syndicate City', and towns near the Canadian border. Bootleggers contrived to supply 'stuff right off the boat', exploiting America's vast coastline. 'The real McCoy', one of several of Prohibition's linguistic contributions, relates to the activities of William J. McCoy who delivered contraband goods of unvarying quality and gained a reputation for absence of

Ramos Gin Fizz

2 parts TANQUERAY® gin
1 part cream
1 egg white
1/2 part lemon juice
1/2 part sugar syrup
5 dashes orange flower water
top with soda

Shake all except soda, very long and very hard. Pour into glass and then fill with soda. Garnish with flower petal.

Invented by the Ramos brothers in New Orleans in 1866. The brothers managed to keep the recipe secret until Prohibition. Enraged by the 'Noble Experiment', they published the recipe – we have been enjoying it ever since. The shaking is the key to dulcifying these diverse ingredients – the legend is that they employed eight large Nubians whose sole job it was to 'shake' the house cocktail!

Prohibition Days: a striking Art Deco sterling silver cocktail shaker (the cap acts as a measure), American, 1930s; a large silver-plated shaker with star motif, produced in Italy for Bonwit Teller, New York, and two distinctive ruby shakers, American, 1930s.

skulduggery. Bill McCoy, from Jacksonville, Florida, retired a millionaire before the repeal of Prohibition in 1933.

A more available source of supply was industrial alcohol, just about drinkable. Liquor distilled from corn sugar, yeasts and malt syrup was obtainable by the late Twenties and 'bath-tub' gin proved one of the simplest spirits to distil at home. The American fascination with trying things out was evidenced by the addition of hitherto unheard of mixers – even medicinal bitters were used – as well as fruit juices and cordials, anything to mask the flavour of the 'bath-tub' gin. Fortuitously, a rash of new cocktails had been invented and, today, around seventy per cent of cocktails ordered across the bar are those introduced during the so-called 'Dry Decade' when the cocktail shaker came of age.

As the 'drys' triumphed and America ran dry, bartenders packed their bags for Europe or the luxury ocean liners (American ships were required to steam across the Atlantic 'dry'). This was the Gilded Age of travel and indulgent and flamboyant design was demanded by the ship owners, not least in the interior appointments to the bar areas on board. In cities across America, the meccas of dining, dancing and drinking closed their doors, to be replaced by a new phenomenon, the 'speakeasy'. The term, in use in America since the 1880s, expressed the supposed secrecy of the transaction, with customer and vendor usually talking in hushed tones about the order. 'Speakeasy' is said to derive from 'speak softly shop', a nineteenth-century English name for a smuggler's house.

One could say that Prohibition drove America to drink. Millions of citizens who associated speakeasies with lowlife, or lived outside the city, drank at home. For others, illicit drinking greatly enhanced the consumption of hard liquor and a fashionable cachet attached to drinking cocktails. Outlaw culture prevailed and, as the Twenties progressed, the business of evading the Eighteenth Amendment and making a mockery of the law became a popular sport. The President of Yale, in his 1922 baccalaureate address, commented, 'the violation of law has never been so general, nor so widely condoned as at present'.

The 'Flapper', a Press term for a high-spirited urban 'modern' on the distaff side, and the well-born Society dame alike, who would never have wished to enter a saloon, now admitted to blissfully 'Making Whoopee', in the words of the song, at speakeasy joints. 'Speaks', serving contraband cocktails – gin was easier to counterfeit than whiskey – as the main icebreaker, now outnumbered pre-Prohibition saloons. Paul Morand's 1930 book *New York* recounts the story of 'An intelligent lady' who 'remarked to me once that Prohibition was very pleasant. "Before it," she said "no decent woman could go into a bar, but now nobody is surprised at our being there".' The fearless could make the rounds of 32,000 speakeasies in New York city alone, redefining the bar-room crawl for all time.

'Hello Suckers!' was the stock in trade cry of the 'Queen of Nightclubs', 'Texas' Guinan. The ex-showgirl numbered Lord and Lady Mountbatten, and Mae West, among her clientele, some of the most illustrious and glamorous ever to haunt the nightclub scene. A British visitor, Stephen Graham, describes a visit in 1927 to one of her emporia (there were several) in *New York Nights*: 'The room is long, but not too long to be homey. No one can be lost in it. There are twenty or thirty tables and a small space in the middle of them for

Sovereigns of the sea: the cocktail bar, with Macassar ebony bar, and observation lounge of the Queen Mary, 1936. The great American adventure, crossing the Atlantic, was considered particularly chic and many added to the infinite pleasures of steaming across by spending time sampling cocktails afloat.

Bourbon Sour

3 parts bourbon
1 part fresh lemon juice
1 part sugar syrup
1 egg white

Shake all ingredients long and hard. Strain into chilled pony glass with a maraschino cherry at the bottom.

A hugely versatile cocktail in which one can use almost any spirit but which works best with the sweet corn whiskey from the Southern United States.

intimate dancing. It is radiantly lighted and yet it is not the light associated with noisy excitement and jazz. There is a low buzz of conversation. Waiters in red-faced uniforms flutter to and fro with silver-topped bottles and elaborately prepared sandwiches.'

Speakeasies were raided with methodical persistence, so that every club had to be carefully guarded against intruders by peepholes and bolted doors. Time and time again well-known premises were padlocked and their proprietors, 'Texas' among them, fined or sent to prison; time and time again the self-same speakeasies reopened. The owners simply wrote off the amount of the fines, or the business losses involved, against the enormous profits made during the successive short spells of existence. Prohibition agent 'Number One' 'Izzy' Einstein, and his partner 'Moe' Smith, disguised as musicians, waiters or out-of-towners in pursuit of their quarry, racked up 4,932 arrests.

Mob controlled, the illicit manufacture and distillation of liquor developed into a major American industry. Officials and federal agents were bribed by the bunch, and a Chicago resident achieved notoriety as the country's best-known gangland boss. The Forest View suburb of Chicago was generally known as 'Caponeville' in deference to 'Al' (Alphonsus) Capone, a hoodlum who ruthlessly eliminated any competition, master-minded the bootleg-related 'St.Valentine's Day Massacre' and is credited with planning the model for gangland organisation. Capone, 'Public Enemy Number One', was charged with violating Prohibition laws in 1931 and started a ten-year sentence, on various counts, the following year. 'The Big Fellow', whose reported annual income was $100,000.000, received a special gift from the 'Outfit' that year in the form of a sterling silver cocktail shaker, famously inscribed ' To A Regular Guy From the Boys 1932'.

The 'Dry' Twenties

The cocktail culture that emerged in the Twenties stood counterpoint to Victorian and Edwardian styles of entertaining. The serving of mixed drinks was the vogue at the convivial mixed receptions of smart hostesses who needed the young to highlight their entertainments, but the servant shortage was a problem for years. Cocktail parties, which could be staged with minimum help, and in all but the smallest apartment, were the perfect solution and rapidly taken up.

The supposedly 'dry' Twenties was a great period for eccentrics. Self expression was the note of the day; the rich, dispensing cocktails from sterling silver shakers, emblematic of status, had more money

The Bramble

2 parts TANQUERAY® gin
¼ part lemon juice
¼ part sugar syrup
½ part crème de mûre

Shake all except mûre. Strain over tumbler of crushed ice and lace with crème de mûre.

Another new drink devised and championed by cocktail guru Dick Bradsell.

In a category of one: a sterling silver shaker inscribed to Al Capone, who achieved world-wide notoriety as a racketeer in Chicago during the Prohibition era. Capone, 'Public Enemy Number One', was sentenced to ten years in prison, but released on health grounds in 1939. He retired to his estate in Florida.

Angels' Delight

1 part TANQUERAY® gin
1 part cointreau
2 parts single/double cream

Shake all and strain into chilled cocktail glass.

Style counts: three elegant silver-plated champagne bottle cocktail shakers surround a brass cocktail set modelled on a Veuve Clioquot bottle, with fitting rose glass flask and matching glasses. The half-bottle to the front is a cigar case.

Brandy Alexander

2 parts Hennessy brandy
1 part crème de cacao
2 parts double cream

Shake all and strain into chilled cocktail glass. Garnish with fresh grated nutmeg.

than ever before and fewer inhibitions about how to express themselves. 'It was better to be modern' wrote Frederick Lewis Allen in *Only Yesterday*, 'everybody wanted to be modern and sophisticated, and smart, to smash the conventions and to be devastatingly frank. And with a cocktail glass in one's hand it was easy at least to be frank'. Boredom was on the way out.

At this point in the evolution of the cocktail shaker the first design patent for a shaker incorporating a 'juicer' was issued, to Louis W. Rice of New York. It was 1924 and these were Prohibition days so the new arrival was described as a 'beverage' shaker.

Meriden in Connecticut, also known as 'Silver City', figures prominently in the overall picture of cocktail shaker history. By 1800, Meriden was already the centre for the production of pewterware. In 1852, several manufacturers had joined together to establish the Meriden Brittania Company, offering affordable pewter, tinware, silverware and 'Brittania' (a pewter-like alloy). Rogers Brothers, one of the first concerns to make electro-plating a working proposition, joined the company ten years later. When a number of New England silversmiths, with the Meriden Brittania Company at the forefront, formed the International Silver Company in 1898, the new organisation, with offices in New York, California, London and elsewhere, retained the names of the subsidiary companies.

Success in promoting their lines – catalogues illustrated a wide range of beverage or mixer sets – was largely generated by the Hotel Division, specialising in flatware and hollowware. The consortium, working to a high level of accomplishment, produced exceptional sterling and silver-plated gifts and in the Twenties and Thirties made a spirited contribution to cocktail shaker design. The International Silver Company held an unchallenged position as the world's largest manufacturer of silverware. One of its divisions, the Derby Plate Silver Company, was responsible for the commission of what is generally claimed to be the first figural cocktail shaker, designed by G. H. Berry in the shape of a golf bag, unveiled in 1926. The eight-piece mixer set contained a golf bag shakers, with simulated cow hide grain, leather straps, stitching and ball bag, and six gold-lined cups on a tray. The sporting set, stamped stock number 1921, was available shortly afterwards with a pouring spout fitted to the bag. George Berry's landmark design, arguably the first of the novelty cocktail shaker genre, conveys a sense of quality and has stood the test of time. Manufacture of both silver-plated versions, made in limited numbers, was discontinued in 1930, and either model is highly sought after today.

Machine Age philosophy: extreme simplification of design in the form of a pair of Chinese cocktail shakers manufactured by Kut Hing, the embodiment of Art Deco design. A combination juicer and strainer are fitted to the lids.

Outstanding among cocktail shakers from the International Silver Company was the replica of the Boston Lighthouse, announced for the 1929 season. America's first lighthouse, on Little Brewster Island in the harbour of the chief fishing port, was built in 1716. (Its original lightkeeper, George Worthylake, tried to make money by running herds of sheep. He was unsuccessful.) The existing Boston Lighthouse, completed in 1859 and preserved as a monument to the Lighthouse Service by a special Act of Congress, provided the model for the International Silver Company design. The mixer, catalogued number 352, was retailed in two sizes; the smaller model fitted with two levels of windows to the surface, and the larger fitted with windows set at three levels around the silver-plated body. A concealed music box could be placed in the base of the larger version. Hosts, by raising the mixer at an appropriate moment, were able to reveal popular tunes such as 'How Dry I Am', or 'Show Me the Way to Go Home'. Surviving examples of the Lighthouse cocktail shakers, expensive when new and of considerable historic interest are, not surprisingly, highly covetable.

As the Twenties roared on, recreation became increasingly hard work. Late hours, martinis mixed by the shakerful, and the heavy punctuated, relentless rhythm of 'Jazzmania' wore out the 'poor little rich girl' of cocktail devotee Noel Coward's song, and her partners. Dancing was still the chief contemporary pastime and the informal cocktail party was established as a popular and fashionable alternative to the dinner party. For the 'bright young set' drinking was no longer considered an exclusively male indulgence, and represented emancipation, a hedonistic lifestyle and conspicuous consumption. In America, those who hoped the prolonged boom, which had delivered economic growth of five per cent annually since 1922, would roar on through to the Thirties would see their hopes swiftly disappointed. It was not war this time, that lay ten years ahead, but the Wall Street crash which was around the next corner. Its effects would be felt severely.

Art Deco in the Machine Age

Meanwhile in Europe, the architectural and decorative style later called Art Deco came to epitomise modern life in the machine age. This was a time of preoccupation with long-distance travel and speed. A new era of record-breaking began and land and air speed record achievements were headline news. The hysterical excitement caused in the United States and the American colony in Paris by Charles Lindbergh's 1927 transatlantic flight was somehow communicated to Britain. American tourists or businessmen, isolated from the Continent during the First World War, had made a wild rush for the boat to Paris following the Armistice. The Little Bar at the Ritz Hotel, situated in the entrance hall and later baptised 'Hemingway' in homage to the writer, patron (and later liberator) who spent the Second World War years as a war correspondent, and Harry's New York Bar, where the mahogany counter and back-bar were shipped over from a pre-Prohibition saloon, were the first to serve chilled American cocktails. A rallying point for thirsty exiles, it was hard to find a free seat at the 'place Vendome', or '5 rue Daunou' (printed on the window of Harry's Bar as 'SANK ROO DOE NOO').

A visit to Britain was almost always included on the itinerary but most Americans spent the majority of their stay in France (a predilection for things French dated from the American Revolution as a sign of complete independence of Britain), or touring Italy. The sophisticated American in Paris learned of European advances in

Bronx

2 parts TANQUERAY® gin
1 part dry vermouth
1 part sweet vermouth
2 parts orange juice

Shake all and strain into chilled cocktail glass. Garnish with cherry or orange wheel.

This is one of the first spirit/juice concoctions, generally now out of favour (like the Borough itself). Invented at the Waldorf-Astoria. Reputedly, customers took one hesitant sip, then finished it with a second.

(Left) Enter the novelty shaker: George Berry's 1926 golf bag design, one of the first figural cocktail shaker ever produced, prefigured the novelty shaker genre. The original version, on the left, was later offered with the fitment of a spout, as shown. Surviving examples are highly sought after.

'The Birds do it, Bees do it' Martini

3 parts TANQUERAY® gin
1 part dry vermouth
dash of cantharis (or other available aphrodisiac)

Shake all well and strain into chilled cocktail glass.

Created by Noel Coward and inspired by the song he sang so well. If cantharis is unavailable then truffles can be substituted.

(Right) To the Lighthouse: silver-plated Lighthouse cocktail shakers manufactured by the International Silver Company, one of the big guns in shaker production, are absolutely in a class of their own. Examples of the larger version are especially rare, with only a handful being recorded.

Boston Iced Tea

1 part Smirnoff vodka
1 part TANQUERAY® gin
1 part white rum
1 part José Cuervo tequila
1 part cointreau
1 part lemon juice
3 parts cold strong tea

Shake all spirits and lemon juice. Strain into highball glass then fill with tea. Garnish with lemon slice.

The father of the now (sadly) ubiquitous Long Island Iced Tea, a drink which became popular during the Noble Experiment of 1919–33.

design directly from the 1925s 'Exposition Internationale des Arts Décoratifs et Industriels Modernes'. The exhibition, originally planned for 1915 but interrupted by the First World War, celebrated a style characterised by a high quality of craftsmanship and innovative forms and coined the phase 'Art Deco'. A showcase for leading magazines like *L'Illustration* or *Arts et Decoration* and, in a futuristic vision, highlighting machine-made objects. Le Corbusier, exhibiting in the *Pavillon de l'Esprit Nouveau*, was described by one source as 'a machine age romantic'. The United States declined their invitation to attend as exhibitors. Herbert Hoover, Secretary for Commerce, and

Of French distinction: a silver cocktail shaker, with twelve hammered silver and shallow-bowled cocktail goblets, c.1930. France was the chief source of European advances in design following the 1925 Paris Exhibition.

later President Hoover, claimed 'nothing new and really original' was ready, but the costs of the international exhibition may have contributed to the decision. Nevertheless, over a hundred delegates crossed the Atlantic to view the Paris Exhibition and Art Deco was exported to America via Press coverage, a major touring exhibition of designs from the show, commencing at the Metropolitan and visiting nine other museums, and the enterprise of the luxury end department stores like Macy's, Lord and Taylor and Saks, glossily packaging Art Deco promotions. Designers like Gilbert Rohde, a contributor to the International Silver Company catalogue, Walter Dorwin Teague and Henry Dreyfuss, visited Europe during 1926–7 and brought the

(Left) True Brits: a selection of English Art Deco silver-plated cocktail shakers from the Thirties. The design for the interior of the Kärtner bar in Vienna by Adolf Loos, 1907, was one of the first true Art Deco designs. Art Deco appeared in Britain around 1928, when it was already declining elsewhere.

Japanese influence: a typical hand-crafted Japanese lacquered cocktail shaker set, c.1935. Lacquer, a hard glossy varnish, is derived from shellac, coloured, and applied to wood or metal accoutrements for decoration (or protection)

(Right) Anglo-Oriental: a fine filigree silver cocktail shaker, fitted with glass liner, 1930s, and a Chinese silver shaker, marked Zeesung silver, featuring a bamboo decorative finish, c.1925. The 1925 Paris Exhibition served as a nursery for new ideas and its influence was widespread.

new ideas to an increasingly style-conscious audience. Interestingly, consultant design was established as a modern professional business at this particular time and its leading members, drawn from architecture, graphic design and advertising, including Norman Bel Geddes, influential in popularising streamlining, Lurelle Guild, Raymond Loewy, and Teague and Dreyfuss, all set up studios around Manhattan. By the end of the pivotal year of 1927, the ground-breaking Art and Color Section of General Motors, 'the beauty parlor', was open under the styling leadership of Harley J. Earl ('I dream automobiles'). Henry Ford, no aesthete, who had laboured to convince his

Objects of desire: a uniquely beautiful cocktail shaker set from Desny of Paris. Masters in the field, the distinctive and original set is one of the finest objects of the period.

associates to prospect for a mass-market utility vehicle, and whose company was engaged in the mass-production of part of American folklore, the serviceable and low-cost Model T 'Tin Lizzie' or 'Flivver' launched a 'designer' Model A Ford in the same year. Overnight, it seemed, the industrial design profession, embracing an exciting range of projects, had emerged. All of this hastened the development of the cocktail shaker; the sharp edge of creative enthusiasm greatly broadened its appeal.

One of the foremost French design firms active in 1927 was the respected house of Desny. Located on the Avenue des Champs-Elysées in Paris and financed by Tricot, the principal designers were Desny and Rene Mauny (or Nauny). The Desny style, which comprised severe geometric forms and plain surfaces, was influenced by the avant-garde painting style of Cubism. Louis Poulain was the resident staff designer. Desny also hired in-vogue designers for their highly praised commissions, and set pencil to paper to produce silverware, lighting fixtures, carpets and murals in the modern spirit. The cultivated modernity of the Desny cocktail shaker set is an exemplar of the style and economy achievable through rational design and has real connoisseur appeal. On Desny's death in 1933, the business ceased. Nauny went on to start the Hippocampe jewellery stores in France. For those who preferred to shop in the rue de la Paix – a de Havilland airliner flew to Paris every two hours from London – a visit to Cartier, the French court jeweller, was considered indispensable. Louis Cartier, who had shown at the Paris Exhibition, was regarded as the genius behind the firm's sought-after *Art Moderne* creations. He employed many fashionable designers, notably Jeanne Toussaint. The Duchess of Windsor commissioned a variety of widely published designs from Cartier, a company reputed to have bought their Fifth Avenue townhouse in New York in exchange for a double string of pearls.

Sales of sterling silver cocktail shakers from Cartier, Asprey, the distinguished English silversmiths established in the eighteenth century and jewellers to the Royal Family since the reign of Queen Victoria, and Tiffany, renowned for the indisputable quality of its sterling silver pieces, were inevitably restricted to a social elite and rank among the best. Of special interest, Louis Comfort Tiffany encouraged well-to-do Americans who acquired their luxury goods in Europe almost exclusively, to recognise that functional and decorative accoutrements could be designed and produced to the same high standards in the United States.

American import: a sterling silver cocktail shaker, patented 1927, rendered with red and black enamel decoration to the body, and supplied with twelve matching enamelled sterling silver glasses. Quality of design and of execution are obvious.

Puiforcat, another exhibitor at the Paris Exhibition and the premier French maker of silver and electro-plate, produced cocktail shakers reflecting extremely high standards of craftsmanship. Jean Puiforçat trained as a silversmith under his father Louis and then studied sculpture before setting up his Paris workshop in 1921. He was influenced by the mathematician Matila Ghyka and contributed greatly to French prestige in design, exhibiting at Grenoble, Milan, Madrid, New York, San Francisco, Buenos Aires and Tokyo. Commissions included dining silver for the Maharajah of Indore, and the great ocean-going French liner 'Normandie', a showcase for Art Deco and launched in 1935. Puiforcat booked his own stand at the 1937 'Exposition Internationale des Arts et Techniques dans la Vie Moderne', the largest of the Paris shows, endorsing 'modern life', with pavilions dedicated to cinema, radio, photography and methods of transport. Asprey's Thirties variety cocktail shakers in the novel form

Nautical influence: desirable silver-plated cocktail shakers in the novel form of ships lanterns from Asprey, c.1935. Few have managed to survive the decades with the original glass liners, and the construction of the framework makes the glass hard to replace.

Daiquiri

2 parts white rum
1 part fresh lime juice
1 part sugar syrup

Shake all and strain into chilled cocktail glass.

Attributed to American engineer Jennings Cox, who supposedly mixed it up to make the local spirit palatable for his bosses. Now transmogrified into the 'frozen fruit' varieties found around the world.

of ship's lanterns, equipped with glass liners in red (for port), green (for starboard) and clear (for the masthead) are now all too rare, and especially appreciated by collectors.

A new element was introduced into cocktail shaker design following the popularity of flying. Great hopes were entertained for the future of civilian flying in the Twenties and many of the adventurous considered the conquest of the air as the most important task of their generation. Flying was popular with both sexes and, as standards of airworthiness in design and maintenance improved, passenger traffic on the 'air expresses' expanded. There was also a marked enthusiasm for private flying. The popular adage ran: 'Be Up to Date and Aviate'.

Aviation has always been a dynamic and dramatically developing industry and in Solingen in Germany, where Luft Hansa enjoyed a monopoly in air transport, the current interest in flying prompted the works of J. A. Henckels to realise their design for a unique portable

bar set in the shape of a monoplane. The travelling bar, all that the discerning collector could wish for, was offered in three sizes, with the detachable wings functioning as flasks. The silver-plated set, produced around 1928, is now a distinguished rarity, and remains an object of admiration among afficionados. The airship, early rival to the aeroplane for supremacy of the air, provided the impetus for the design of one of the finest cocktail shakers ever produced. Henckels works again showed what could be expected from their Solingen team.

Count Ferdinand Graf von Zeppelin of Friedrichshafen led the world in airship-building and developed one of the most promising visions of future mass air transportation. He was awarded a patent for his rigid 'dirigible' (steerable) vessel in 1898. Zeppelin No.1 made its debut in 1901, and Deutsche Luftschiffahrts AG (Delag), founded

Made in Germany: two studies of J.A. Henckels' outstanding airplane travelling bar set. The exploded view illustrates the components – internal flask, a pair of hip flasks, four cups, spoons, strainer, funnel corkscrew and olive box. One of the very best looking of them all, the classic design has cast its spell over top collectors. This is the rare 12″ version, one of very few examples known.

Not a shaker in sight: a smiling Count von Zeppelin takes off. His Graf Zeppelin airship served Moselle and Rhine wines, champagne and cognac but it was too early for cocktails.

Clover Club

2 parts TANQUERAY® gin
1 part lemon juice
½ part grenadine
1 egg white

Shake all very hard and strain into chilled cocktail glass. Garnish with a lemon wheel.

Supposedly invented at the Clover Club in Philadelphia, but no 'official' record of it can be found.

in 1909, was the world's first airline company. A service was inaugurated between Lake Constance and Berlin in the following year and, with the support of the Emperor, and a national fund-raising appeal, the Count's perseverance was rewarded. He built and experimented with new types of more and more advanced large rigid airships. From such beginnings, came the legendary Graf Zeppelin, launched in 1928 and christened LZ-127.

The splendid airship, at least the equal of Concorde in terms of celebrity, demonstrated the wide choice of routes available to a vast dirigible with such a tremendously long range and made the first ever transatlantic flight. In an outstanding nine-year career, including a heroic four-stage round-the-world journey in 1929, the Graf Zeppelin completed 590 successful flights and caught the public imagination.

Its successor, the giant Hindenburg, LZ-129, is credited with serving the first in-flight chilled cocktail, conveniently known as the LZ-129. Shaken, not stirred, the gin-based cocktail was presented in a frosted glass. (Drinks carts were rolling down the aisles on American passenger aircraft by the Thirties.) The ill-starred Hindenburg was lost in flames on approach to Lakehurst, New Jersey, in 1937. The Graf Zeppelin was decommissioned with the coming of war.

The aerodynamic shaker from Solingen, very much part of the Zeppelin legend, was also on sale in 1928. Finished in silver-plate, available in three sizes, and imported into the United States in the main by the Rodak Import and Export Corporation, New York, the sets came with their own leather travelling case. The exclusive Zeppelin cocktail shaker – familiarity has never dimmed its magic – is regarded by many as the ultimate collectable in the field.

It was in 1928 that Lurelle Guild produced his striking cocktail shaker set in the dominant style of a skyscraper, released under the International Silver Company banner by subsidiary Wilcox Silver Plate Company as beverage sets number 5833 and 5840. William Lescaze, a Swiss-born architect also active in the decorative arts and metalwork, and American George Howe, set about producing the first modern skyscraper in Philadelphia in 1929. A great, newly rich nation's contribution to design, the skyscraper expressed wealth and power, and was the role model for forms and ornamentation.

Le Corbusier elected to use a photograph of the Barclay-Verey (telephone company) Building for the 1927 English language edition of *Towards a New Architecture*, and the skyscraper motif is pronounced in *The Metropolis of Tomorrow*, by Hugh Ferris, daring to peer into the future in 1929. The Channin Building (1927–9) in New York was called by one commentator 'the first real skyscraper to be started in the Twenties'. Walter Chrysler, who banged the door on the way out of the General Motors Building (out of that bang was made the Chrysler Corporation), commissioned William Van Arlen for the Chrysler Building, transforming the Gotham (home to King Kong) skyline on its completion in 1929 and suggesting a rocket-ship ready for lift-off. The skyscraper image is sustained in the work of Raymond Loewy, destined to be a major styling influence at Studebaker, a one hundred per cent American automobile, and was conspicuous in the design of domestic interiors. Many consumers, unable to assimilate the new functionalist innovations in furniture design, proved more receptive when the same principles were applied to domestic objects. Skyscrapers reached their heyday in the following decade.

Floridita

2 parts light rum
$\frac{1}{2}$ part fresh lime juice
$\frac{1}{2}$ part sweet vermouth
1 dash white crème de cacao
1 dash grenadine

Shake all and strain into chilled cocktail glass. Garnish with lime wheel.

The house cocktail from Havana's famous El Floridita which, together with head bartender Constantino Ribailagua (and a little help from one E. Hemingway), laid claim to originating several classic cocktails.

The shaker that made history: the distinctive perfectionist stamp of J. A. Henckels is evident in these two illustrations of the meticulously executed Zeppelin cocktail shaker set, produced at the same time as the aircraft travelling bar set. One of the most coveted sets of them all, collectors are passionate about the elegantly shaped Zeppelins from Solingen.

Charlie Lindbergh Cocktail

1 part TANQUERAY® gin
1 part kina lillet
2 dashes orange juice
2 dashes pricota

Shake well and serve in cocktail glass. Squeeze lemon peel on top.

The first solo transatlantic flight celebrated in a cocktail. 'Be Up To Date and Aviate', as the popular slogan ran.

Lurelle Van Arsdale Guild was one of the leading players among industrial designers. He studied Fine Art at Syracuse; there followed a brief spell as an actor before he turned, like Bel Geddes and Russel Wright, to set designing. He collaborated with his wife, Louise Eden Guild, on drawings, and undertook magazine illustration. By the time he first imagined his skyscraper cocktail shaker he was riding the crest of a wave, with over 1,000 designs a year or more on the blocks in his Fifth Avenue headquarters. His drawings, based on a sound knowledge of mechanical engineering, could be used without modification by his client's staff. Guild, an experienced metalworker, who also wrote authoritatively about antique furniture, built working models and sometimes tested market response to his household objects by displaying them in department stores. He asserted, without a trace of self doubt, that 'Beauty does not always sell'.

Bygone age: Henckels elected to produce a whole range of travelling bar accessories and there is an unmistakable touch of quality about the Solingen maker's products. A fine set of 'binocular' drinking flasks, equipped with miniature shot cups and funnels and supplied in a fitted case.

The makers reissued Guild's graceful cocktail shaker in 1934, with colour adding another dimension. There was a new tray for the 'Smart gifts for Smart people' and the set was promoted as 'the ultimate in gifts for the bride'. The cocktail shaker has been an adjunct to history for over a hundred years, be it artistic, social or literary. In Mary McCarthy's best-selling novel, *The Group*, Kay – one of the eight Vassar women of the Class of 1933 whose lives are followed for seven years after graduation – selects a Russel Wright Cocktail Hour set as her wedding gift.

Lurelle Guild, whose enthusiasm for early American crafts led remarkably to the moving and restoration of an early American village from New Hampshire in Darien, Connecticut, where he lived, furnished over fifty designs to the catalogues of Chase Brass and Copper, at Waterbury. A long association with Kensington, a division of Alcoa (Aluminum Company of America), situated in New Kensington, Pennsylvania, commenced in 1934, when Guild accepted a commission to create a new giftware line in 'Kensington' metal, an aluminium alloy. In 1936, he applied streamline – a word of nautical origin – techniques for Kensington's skyscraper cocktail service. *Design Magazine* recorded its approval: 'the simplicity of

Cowboy Martini

3 parts TANQUERAY® gin
$\frac{1}{4}$ part sugar syrup
10 whole fresh mint leaves
orange twist

Place mint in bottom of shaker and cover with ice. Add gin and then shake very vigorously to allow ice to pummel mint. Strain through fine strainer into chilled glass then grate orange rind over surface.

Another cocktail contrived in London by Dick Bradsell.

Overlapping contemporaries: a nickel-plated travelling cocktail set, with cocktail shaker, flask, cups, strainer, funnel and measure, again from Henckels in Germany – and a set containing three glass flasks, also nickel-plated, English c.1930.

form, enhanced by careful use of ornament, characterises the discrimination of the modern industrial design'. Interest has focused on Lurelle Guild's stylish cocktail shakers and his benchmark designs are increasingly hard to find.

'MB Means Best' was the Manning Bowman trademark in the Twenties. The revered Meriden concern, founded in 1832, with a reputation for quality and individuality in design, stressed its commitment to the cocktail shaker market with unashamedly elitist, and expensive, mixer sets. Towards the end of the Twenties, Manning Bowman had perfected the chromium-plating process and introduced Aranium, 'the plate that does not tarnish'. Chromium, the silver-like metallic element obtained from chrome ironstone by smelting, was detected by the French chemist, Vacquelin, in 1798.

(Left) The sky's the limit: Lurelle Guild's immaculate silver-plated skyscraper cocktail set, with matching monogrammed 'C' cups, which was designed for the International Silver Company in 1932. Guild was a leading figure among a group of talented and highly qualified designers drawn to industrial design.

(Right) Gyro-practice: clear and frosted glass skyscraper cocktail shakers, a gyroscope glass rack – standard barware at the fabled Rainbow Room in New York – and an unusual martini cocktail shaker decorated with sterling silver. London clay, unlike Manhattan Island, would not support skyscrapers and a limit was set for the heights of the buildings. Gyroscopic racks allowed even the most inebriated to serve cocktails without spillage.

All American: a chromium capstan winch cocktail shaker, the underside inscribed with fourteen recipes, Foreman Bros., 1930s; a 'Tippler' aluminium and plastic shaker by West Blend Aluminium, 1940s; a chromium-plated fire extinguisher style shaker, c.1935; a Manning Bowman walnut-topped chrome shaker, and an aluminium and Bakelite Ritz shaker with spiral decorations, 1940s.

It was finally made available commercially, following use for projectile coverings during the First World War, in 1925. Manning Bowman claimed that its 'persistent brilliance' and resistance to corrosion made chromium the ideal finish for the cocktail shaker. 'Even the teetotaller could not help admiring the beauty inherent in the design' promised the lyrical commentary from the makers. The straight-limbed cocktail shakers, maintaining the tradition of excellence always associated with the name, were found in the mirrored and illuminated interiors of the best cocktail-cabinets, a piece of furniture symbolising modernity and marking the acceptance of drinking as a respectable social activity. Soon, however, an unparalleled upheaval would make it altogether impossible for American manufacturers to continue to maintain a product line without compromise with the times.

The Bonanza Years of the Twenties in America, driven by rampant speculation, must have looked to some as if they would last forever, but in August 1929 share prices began to decline greatly. In October came the sudden end of the Hoover prosperity boom when the whole Wall Street stock market collapsed. The American public had been interesting itself in the market and plunging in with enthusiastic ignorance. Financiers, exploiting the bullish trend, drove up the nominal value of stock to the highest figure possible, in order to unload on amateur speculators to the best advantage. They were too successful. When they pulled out, leaving the market to find its own level, it crashed dramatically. On 'Black Tuesday', 29 October 1929, sixteen million shares were traded and investments went down the drain. Panic continued: hundreds of thousands of Americans lost their spare cash and then rushed to the banks to be sure of their capital. The surge broke the smaller banks and they, in turn, dragged down many of the larger banks. Companies slid down the slope to liquidation – nearly a third of all American businesses failed – and twelve million were thrown out of employment. The effects of the Wall Street crash could not be localised. No money was forthcoming for foreign goods, or lending to foreign powers, and a decrease in American orders and the general disorganisation of world markets led to a sharp rise in unemployment, particularly in Germany and Britain. The threat of a slump seemed inevitable; the 'Roaring Twenties', carefree decade of a new peace, was over.

Chic, fashionable hotels with fancy addresses come and go. But for those looking for *luxe* there is always the Savoy, one of London's enduring landmarks (its view of the River Thames memorably captured by Claude Monet). As Americans back home struggled to balance the books, convivial Americans in Europe headed for the American Bar at the Savoy Hotel, known to their liquor-deprived countrymen as the '49th State'. The Savoy Hotel was designed by T.E. Colcutt and opened in 1899. Outside those swing doors, on the fore-court, is the only street in Britain where traffic must keep to the right. César Ritz, his name a synonym for elegance and luxury, was the first manager of the hotel and Auguste Escoffier ('the king of chefs, and the chef of kings') presided over the kitchens. Together, these two legendary figures created a card index of the 'Ritz and famous', and converted London society to the practice of dining out. As banker Otto Kahn remarked, with Ritz and Escoffier in town, London was 'a place worth living'. Well put.

In 1920, Harry Craddock, a young American barman, came to London to practise the art of mixing drinks at the hotel. He became head bartender in 1925 and, five years later, mixed his own compilation, *The Savoy Cocktail Book*. The cocktail age was in full swing by 1930 in the United Kingdom but for many imbibers the general rule, like chemistry before the periodic table, was 'mix a few things together and occasionally there's a puff of smoke'. Craddock's compendium was all you needed to know about cocktail recipes ('A Few Hints for the Young Mixer'), and, still in print, remains a standard work. Harry Craddock, the first president of the British Bartender's Guild, was still practising the art of mixing drinks at the Savoy in 1939. All the established classics in his mixology bible are on the menu today. The dry martini remains the most popular cocktail.

The Savoy was the first abode to popularise dining with dancing, intriguing and attracting guests by lowering, or raising, the dance-floor. A typical evening out for the affluent in London in 1930 might consist of cocktails – Britain's cocktail age was very London biased – at the American Bar, followed by a four- or five-course dinner (there were numerous courses, but portions were smaller). After supper, the evening could wind up with dancing at one of the many nightclubs – dance-band leaders, who enjoyed a huge personal following, sold records in the hundreds of thousands – or at one of the bottle parties dotted around the West End.

It is true that in Britain at the start of the new decade the cocktail age was confined to the select few – a bottle of gin approximated the pay of an unskilled worker for a week – but the Depression did little to halt the steady advance of living standards which had been so marked a feature of twentieth-century British life, although great

Debonaire

2 parts Oban single malt
1 part canton ginger liqueur

Shake all and strain into chilled cocktail glass.

One of the very few drinks that uses a single malt in what some would call heretical fashion. This is a new take on the Whisky Mac with far more refined ingredients.

The Monseigneur Bar: bar staff were expected to observe rigid rules of conduct and to speak only when spoken to and answer questions civilly and briefly. No matter how well a barman knew a customer, pointing out his drunken antics of the night before could prove fatal.

contrasts between rich and poor existed. The cocktail craze, elevated to a plinth adjacent to its American counterpart, honoured an important principle in the world of drink – the Frivolity Rule. Amusements for the pretty and fashionable, style-setting celebrities and the new rich (fortunes were gained and lost during 1914–18), were much written about and a torrent of ink was spilt by columnists on the glamour of cocktail parties. The stories delighted a generation.

Gin, without a prefix, now meant London dry gin, more concentrated, fast emerging as the leader of the field in the quality stakes.

One of the traditions of the American Bar at the Savoy was the preparation of cocktails, mainly short and mainly alcoholic, for special occasions. History does not record the popularity of the gin-based Prohibition cocktail but Napoleon and Salome – a little name dropping is irresistible – princesses and movie stars, avenues in Paris, the Turf and the motor car, all provided inspiration for cocktail wizardry. The gin-based Rolls-Royce cocktail was named after the makers of 'The Best Car in the World', hand-finished under the managing directorship of Claude Johnson (known as the 'hyphen' in Rolls-Royce). Jack Barclay, speed king and retailer of the famous marque, specified a walnut cocktail cabinet, backgammon board, smoker's companion to the armrest (Havana cigar compartment), and the American novelty of a glass roof, for his Rolls-Royce Wraith model, registered JB1. Captain Woolf Barnato, another competitive driver, who once raced and comfortably beat the 'Blue Train' from the Riviera, was chairman of Rolls-Royce rival, Bentley, in 1930. 'Babe' Barnato's family fortunes were made in the diamond fields of South Africa and the 'Barnato millions', headline news at the time, were finally settled in his favour, following a seven-year lawsuit. A man about town when in the mood, a man of action in another, Barnato was the

49th State': Martyn Roland and bar-man behind the Savoy Hotel bar in 1927. Three years later, head bar-tender Harry Craddock published his landmark *The Savoy Cocktail Book*, very much part of cocktail legend and still in print today. The 'guests' are Osbert Sitwell, novelist, critic and poet, and his brother Sacheverell, poet and art historian. Edith, their older sister, was one of the great English eccentrics.

quintessential international sportsman, financier and playboy. The junction of Grosvenor Square and Carlos Place was known to London cab drivers as 'Bentley corner' and at one of his renowned Mayfair cocktail parties, 'Bentley Boys' and their guests were greeted by waiters wearing racing kit, complete with crash helmets. Table decor was a miniature banked Brooklands race track and a note pinned to the menu advised: 'Before parking his or her chassis, each driver should ensure that his or her carburettor is flooded with at least two cocktails'. Barnato's name is inseparably linked to the race-bred Bentleys, whose exploits at Le Mans have passed into history. The Rolls-Royce cocktail appears on page 136 and the Bentley cocktail on page 27 of Harry Craddock's book.

There is a potential magic in the art of preparing a cocktail and, in July 1930, the first International Cocktail Competition was announced in London, with the lofty intention of discovering 'the top mixer of them all and reveal his true greatness to the world'. Master mixologists lined up for this arresting event in September, won by Tom Buttery's 'The Golden Dawn Cocktail'. Incidentally, his employers, the Berkeley Hotel in London, proposed a menu to attract those of a deal-making disposition, 'With appropriate wines' said Phillip Ferraro, the restaurant's director, 'that menu will soften the heart of the hardest hearted businessman and put him into an excellent frame of mind for negotiations.' Tycoons please step forward.

'Some cocktails should be stirred – not shaken!' recommended Chase Brass and Copper in their literature. The Connecticut manufacturer, who made industrial metal products including bar stock, set up a speciality design division under Rodney Chase, the son of the president, around 1927. The distinguishing Chase trademark, a centaur with drawn bow, made its debut in the following year. The Depression, a failure both of capitalism and economic theory, disposed of a number of makers and hard times compelled others in the consumer goods market to originate new ideas and new products. Chase reached the prudent conclusion that there was little to be lost in promoting a decorative giftware line, and their first known catalogue appeared in 1933, the year Henry Laylon joined the Waterbury company. Laylon, resident designer and later director of

Edward of the Ritz: César Ritz, the famous Swiss-born hotel proprietor, contributed importantly to the success of dining out in London and once famously remarked 'The customer is never wrong'. Monarch later catalogued a 'Ritz' cocktail shaker.

Measuring up: a set of six cocktail jiggers in the shape of nuts and bolts, English, 1930s. No bartender is so good that he can mix consistently good cocktails without measuring.

Gilded age: a superior cocktail shaker finished in silver and distinguishable by its domed lid and fluted design to the neck, English, 1934; another English silver shaker, with wide-banded decoration on cap and neck from H.A. (Atkin Brothers, silversmiths), 1938; a silver-plated version from Maple of London c.1925; a ruby glass baluster-shaped model with recipes, c.1938, and duck and snail cocktail stick holder, French, 1930s.

French connection: a vertically cut heavy silver crystal cocktail shaker, with silver-mounted cap and strainer, c. 1935, a superb crystal shaker, the body to Balthus pattern, the shoulder and cap in silver gilt, bearing a Minerva emblem and produced in the late Thirties by Baccarat, under Georges Chevalier, and a bevelled glass, silver-topped shaker, c. 1925.

Gimlet

2 parts TANQUERAY® gin
¾ part Rose's lime cordial

Shake all and strain into chilled cocktail glass. Garnish with lime wedge.

Invented by the British Royal Navy for medicinal purposes. The vitamin C in Rose's lime cordial helped prevent scurvy. Sir Thomas Gimlette, Naval surgeon, believed neat gin 'clouded the minds of the new recruits'. He was probably right.

design, convinced Chase management of the wisdom of working in partnership with the engineering department, resulting in the development of cost-effective designs. He put all his energy and ambition behind this activity – he was twenty-two years old at the time – and signed freelance designers such as Walter von Nessen, Russel Wright and Lurelle Guild. Chase products, admired for their inventive advertising and marketing techniques, became a household name in America.

It is more than right that Walter von Nessen has been given his due among collectors. Born in Berlin, and a prolific designer of great integrity, he founded the Nessen Studio for design and manufacture in 1927. (His famed swing-arm lamp, still in use today in various configurations, was introduced in this decisive year for industrial design.) In 1930, with a general down turn in trading evident, he announced the expansion of his New York studio. Architects, designers and retailers were among his impressive list of clients, and his critically esteemed Stirring Cocktail Mixer featured in Chase's 1937 line-up.

Russel Wright – it is believed he dropped the second 'l' from his Christian name when a stationery order was printed with a single 'l' – was one of the youngest of the new breed of design consultants.

Gibson

3 parts TANQUERAY® gin
¼ part dry vermouth
2 cocktail onions

Shake and strain into chilled cocktail glass. Garnish with cocktail onions.

Stories of the Gibson's creation are many: Charles Dana Gibson was an artist specialising in 'pin-up' girls. One night he challenged the bartender in the Players Club to make 'a better martini' and he garnished it with two onions to remind the drinker of the breasts of the girls he drew. Alternatively, it was invented by twin girls who drank them in Chicago (twin olives for twins); or, by a cardsharp who drank water and had the bartender garnish it with onions to allow him to recognise it.

Shine of the times: a cherished and polished 'Thirst Extinguisher' from Asprey, one of the very costliest of cocktail shakers when introduced into the range in 1932, and now appreciated and highly collectable. Standards of workmanship are beyond reproach.

'Come Aboard for Cocktails': sailor signalling from the deck – a sought-after American glass shaker, 1940s – a glass shaker, with silver-plated top, showing the Supermarine S5 aircraft and two glasses decorated with a Zeppelin and a monoplane, English, 1930s; a boxed set of six cocktail sticks, hallmarked Birmingham, 1935, and a pair of caliper-shaped ice tongs from the workshops of Hagenauer, the Vienna metalsmiths, c. 1935.

Red Snapper

3 parts TANQUERAY® gin
5 parts tomato juice
spices to taste including celery salt, fresh black pepper, Tabasco, horse-radish
$\frac{1}{2}$ part lemon juice
$\frac{1}{2}$ part dry sherry

Build all in shaker. Shake once only. Strain into high-ball glass. Garnish with lime wedge or squeeze of and/or celery stalk and twist of fresh black pepper.

The original 'Bloody Mary' invented by Pete Petiot in Paris, 1924 – 'Bloody' came later. Social changes meant the word lost its offensiveness.

A friend of the playwright Thornton Wilder, Wright started his career working for the P. T. Barnum of industrial design, Norman Bel Geddes, as a scenic designer. His decorative break came in 1927 – casting miniature versions of his stage sets. In his own workshop in New York, he designed and produced items in spun aluminium, a malleable, and affordable, alternative to chrome, copper or silver. (Wright's sterling silver pieces acknowledged the influence of the French metalsmith, Jean Puiforcat.) The first of the new wave of industrial designers to be cited in product advertising, his spun aluminium 'Cocktail Hour' set – the neck of the cocktail shaker wrapped in cork to prevent chilling the hand – is both collectable and valuable.

Expertise in cocktail shaker design was also embodied in the work Howard F. Reichenbach, busy at Chase planning sales, working as development, and product, designer and succeeding in producing the Gaiety cocktail shaker which brought rising sales totals in 1933. The 'Gaiety', in the words of its designer, was 'a shaker of superior convenience, appearance and effectiveness, constructed with

Golf-minded: a silver pocket hip flask, embossed with golfing scene, 1930s; a glass cocktail shaker with golfer in mid-swing design, 1950s; a set of golf club stirrers in golf ball base, 1930s; golf club stirrers in a top hat by Chase, 1940s, and a set of golf ball cocktail sticks, 1930s. All American.

particular reference to preventing the escape of any fluid, no matter how violently it is shaken'. Black enamel bands on the chrome-plated surface added distinction and, from year two, red, green, white or blue bands were offered as alternatives. A cocktail shaker, to quote the brochure, 'Entirely modern in appearance' and retaining 'all the desirable features of an old-fashioned shaker', together with cups and a tray designed by Harry Laylon, the popular 'Gaiety' was marketed as the Holiday Cocktail Set. The six-piece shaker set was one of the premiums offered to smokers of Kool cigarettes. Smoke 650 packs (sic), collect the coupons and the 'Happy Hour' was all yours. 'For moderns on your list, a clever cocktail set' was how Macy's described Reichenbach's Blue Moon eight-piece set, with Laylon designed cups and ring tray. Patented in 1934, and finished in polished chromium, the 'Blue Moon' was fitted with a glass, or less costly Catalin, stopper.

Catalin, like Bakelite, a thermosetting plastic (from the Greek, Plasticos, to form or to mould) was the trademark of the American Catalin Company, established in New York in 1927. A cast phenolic

Women behaving differently: with the battle of the suffragettes decades behind them, much of the nation's workforce female, and married couples now thought of as partners, the position of women in the Thirties was outwardly one of greater freedom.

To shake, or not to shake: for those who hold it necessary to stir, a gleaming sterling silver cocktail pitcher from Tiffany, late 1930s, and a pair of silver-plated martini pitchers and stirrers, English, 1940s. One commentator cautioned 'stirring is prescribed in certain mixtures which are known to take harm from violent agitation'.

resin, Catalin (motto: 'The Gem of Modern Industry') was available in a rainbow of colours. The more common form was Bakelite, the trade name used by Leo H. Baekeland, the Belgian chemist and inventor. A patent was received in 1907 for his phenol-formaldehyde brittle plastic (advertised as 'The Material of a Thousand Uses'). Its first general application was in the electrical industry. Both resins were adopted by contemporary designers, conjuring up appropriately modern symbols when consumer interest in twentieth-century technologies was rising.

'I work on the principle that nothing that can be done by machine should be done by hand' wrote Jacques-Emile Ruhlmann, an indication of the interest in machinery and progress of the prominent French designer of interiors and furnishings. In 1929, writing in *A Shopper's Guide to Paris*, the American authors Therese and Louise Bonney commented: 'Where France leads the way today in decorative art, and centres its creations in Paris, possibly another country will lead in 1940. America should since it is here that the machine age, the inspiration for most creative effort today, is developing the possibilities.' The considerable interest aroused by the new materials such as plastic – there were even Bakelite coffins – and chromium and aluminium, coupled with a passion for the machine, led to the

Bakelite: two examples of 'The Master Incolor Cocktail Shaker Set' moulded in Urea-formaldehyde for William Gill by Thomas de la Rue, c.1935. Cap rotates to reveal recipes. A large strainer was fitted for 'perfect mixing' and a 'magical spout that ensures no spillage'.

The Jongle Martini

4 parts TANQUERAY® gin
dash dry vermouth
splash of mango juice

Shake gin and pour into chilled cocktail glass. Add splash of mango juice and make a twist from the rind.

Jongle is French for jungle. This martini was supposedly inspired by Rousseau, famous for his tropical paintings. He had never seen a jungle and instead sought inspiration from the Paris botanical gardens.

emergence in the early Thirties of the Moderne, Modernistic or Jazz Moderne style, a mix of Art Deco and the Modern. The futuristic style reflected the mass production techniques pioneered in the United States and the dynamism of contemporary American culture. Industrial design was one of the most distinctive cultural forms of the twentieth century and the leading edge design consultants who elected to work in the new style exercised an important influence as design progressed to a machine aesthetic. The whole scene was given the seal of modernity by streamlining.

Streamlining – known in the wind tunnel as aerodynamics – is the contouring of an object to reduce its resistance to motion (or drag)

The MacMartini

4 parts TANQUERAY® gin
3 drops of Johnnie Walker
Black Label

Stir all the ingredients
together and strain into
chilled cocktail glass.

*Invented by Max Morgan
('Mad Max') in Inverness in
1948. Inspired by hearing a
rendition of 'When the
Saints Come Marching in',
memorably performed by
six Scottish pipers.*

through a stream of air. Already in use in the early part of the twentieth century on other objects than planes or airship-gondolas, notably on open motor cars, the emphasis was on smooth, enveloping forms. The carefully determined streamlining approach, was applied to all manner of decorative arts and is particularly apparent in the design of the cocktail shaker, as subject to period affectations as any work of furniture or decoration.

The Thirties was a great time for the cocktail shaker. Never before had the tastes of the buyer been catered for so widely, and versions of the utmost variety and interest evolved throughout the period. The years 1930–41 must be accounted the golden age of the cocktail shaker.

Glass Production

The American glass industry was stimulated in the trough of the Depression to meet the challenge to manufacture glass inexpensively. The practical and decorative use of glass goes back as far as recorded history, but traditional hand-blown, or cut processes, were time-consuming and costly. To their credit, the makers devised a machine-made method employing tank moulds. Patterns were etched in acid, or carved directly into the pressing mould. Machines could also enamel or silk-screen designs on to the glass. The characteristic colours were created by the addition of metallic elements such as manganese, copper, cobalt and chromium, as well as non-metallic agents. The handsome Hawkes glass cocktail shaker, etched with vertical lines, was selected along with a Heisey glass shaker, to represent the best in affordable American modern design by the Museum of Modern Art in New York in 1940.

Hazel Atlas impressed with their 1930 Sportsman Series of glass cocktail shakers and top marks go to John Held Jnr for his excellent contribution to the life and times of the shaker. Held, who invoked the giddy age between the wars for his glass shaker design, illustrated Scott Fitzgerald's *Tales of the Jazz Age* and conveyed, like the author, the spirit of the time. He drew the pictures for Emily Post's delightfully-titled *How to Behave – Though a Debutante*, and his skills were in demand on humorous magazines like *Live*, and on *Vanity Fair*, devoted to 'those things which make the smart world smart'. Major glassware companies like Heisey, Cambridge, Imperial and Duncan Miller, by a coincidence of several factors and social developments, had produced a noteworthy series of cocktail shakers

A touch of glass: a large cobalt blue glass cocktail shaker with inlaid sterling silver hunting scene and similar English and American examples from the Thirties. The major glass companies, anticipating the end of Prohibition, geared up for repeal by producing shakers, pitchers, decanters and ice buckets.

and manufactured more glass during the recession than at any other period in the industry's history. The virtues of Depression era glass are demonstrated by their continuing status among collectors. Values have risen dramatically.

The time-honoured Cambridge Glass Company of Ohio, experienced in the production of transparent coloured glass and makers of fine crystal, spared nothing when they embarked on the manufacture of their series of etched cocktail shakers and the Rose Point, Gloria, Diane and Wildflower patterns are readily commended by seasoned collectors. Cambridge supplied cocktail shaker blanks, a common practice, for other firms to silk-screen and finish. Typical of such alliances was the one made with Farber Brothers of New York.

Louis and Harry Farber are chiefly remembered for their profitable collaboration with Cambridge on a line of chromium gifts with removable coloured glass inserts. Chromium-plating first came into general use in the middle of the Twenties and Farber Brothers registered the trademark 'Kromekraft' for their 'non-tarnishing' giftware. The S. W. Farber Company, also based in New York, and operated by their brother Simon, was unconnected; products of S. W. Farber are stamped 'Farberware'. Both concerns prospered and

The Picasso Martini

5 parts TANQUERAY® gin
$^1\!/_2$ part Hennessy cognac
$^1\!/_2$ cups espresso coffee
sugar to taste

Shake all and strain into chilled cocktail glass.

Picasso's favourite. He insisted that the balance between the caffeine stimulation and the alcohol's sedative effect produced temporary but nervous euphoria – 'like making love on wet paint'.

Indescribably blue: cobalt blue glass recipe cocktail shakers. Chrome-topped model, c.1938; skyscraper version with horizontally-ribbed design, 1935, and diamond-shaped motif shaker from the same period. Glass manufacture was successfully increased during the Depression era.

chose to broaden their product base during the Thirties by introducing constantly good, but conventionally styled, cocktail shakers, in opposition to the design trends of the day. The two companies, not as adventurous as some American counterparts, were never tempted to make innovations for their own sake. For sheer conservatism, the Farber family could not be beaten.

The year 1933 marked a dramatic turning point for the cocktail shaker but before we pick up the Prohibition story again, the spotlight turns on Chicago and 'A Century of Progress', an exhibition which opened, with the lights turned on with energy from the star

(Left) 'Jazz Age': John Held Jnr, the American cartoonist and illustrator, depicted the Bright Young Things on this exceedingy rare cocktail shaker. Held, an amiable satirist, created immortal characters and mocked the foibles of the time. He epitomised the 'Jazz Age' trend of the Twenties, when smart folk in America lived well. His famous comic strips of the era ended with the Wall Street Crash in 1929.

(Right) Thirst quenchers: a silver-plated fire extinguisher-design 'Thirst Extinguisher'. F.C. & Co., English, c.1930; a matching green glass shaker containing recipes for twenty-four classic cocktails, American, 1930s; a similar example, a silver-plated Art Deco shaker, with ribbed detail on the shoulder, French, 1930s, and a stylish Art Deco silver-plated octagonal version, with stepped base, English, 1930s.

Arcturus, in May 1933. While America, as we have seen, was not quarantined from European design influences, this single event was demonstrably effective in popularising the 'streamlined Moderne' style in the country. Chicago provided the perfect environment for the exhibition: in 1928 'A Century of Progress' was organised as a non-profit-making corporation with the objective of staging a World's Fair in 1933, whose theme was the progress of civilisation during the century of Chicago's existence. Stirring stuff, and as if to prove that it had a monopoly on the future, it drew 39 million visitors (it was extended into 1934) – the first time in history a fair in the United

Thirties conventional: a ribbed-design porcelain shaker with recipes on the lid, and a traditional chrome and Bakelite model, also from Kromekraft. The S.W. Farber Co., run independently by another Farber brother, used the trademark 'Farberware'.

Shakers galore: the shaker to the right is inscribed 'Happy Days at the Century of Progress, Chicago 1934'. Chicago was the home of an inventive and prolific school of architect designers.

States had paid for itself. The World's Fair changed the attitude of millions of citizens to mass-produced objects and inspired the Aluminium Products Company, La Grange, to release 'Happy Days at the Century of Progress, Chicago 1934', a design described by one expert as ' a swell little cocktail shaker'. ('Happy Days' was a reference to the Democratic Party campaign song in the run-up to the 1932 Presidential election.)

It was patently sensible to repeal Prohibition. Federal government support for the measure varied considerably but generally the ruling was enforced where the people were sympathetic. Cities were strongly

opposed to enforcement. There is much evidence that Prohibition supporters, rocked by the rise in the illicit production and sale of alcohol (attorney turned bootlegger George Remus bought nine distilleries and amassed a fortune before he was caught), gangland excess and the patronage of the speakeasy, increasingly viewed Prohibition as a restriction on individual freedom.

The Depression put the severest brake on the economy and opponents could argue persuasively that people were deprived of jobs and the government of revenue. (Mabel Walker Willebrandt, in charge of liquor law, had resigned in 1928 to act as attorney for the wine trade.) In 1932 the Democratic Party, running on a platform calling for

Paint it black: a very stylish Art Deco black-purple glass shaker, American, 1930s; a rare black glass skyscraper with horizontal ribbing and gold painted bands, and a large jigger and stirrers, the perfect bar companions.

repeal, one of the key issues on the campaign trail, energetically promoted a 'New Deal' of bank support and Federal spending to stimulate production. Franklin Delano Roosevelt's landslide victory made certain that it was only a matter of time before repeal was achieved. At last deliverance came on 5 December 1933, when the 21st Amendment to the Constitution, repealing the 18th, was ratified. Liquor control came to be determined more and more at local level. The cocktail shaker was finally allowed out of hiding.

The new President 'FDR' was rumoured to have motored around the golf courses with a silver cocktail shaker and liked his martinis made with a teaspoon of brine. Mixing his first legal martini in the White House and toasting the repeal of Prohibition, he called on the Cocktail Nation to practise moderation. Roosevelt's informal afternoon gatherings for secretaries and staff in Washington where cocktails were preferred, were likened by the President to 'the Children's Hour'.

So ended the Noble Experiment. What happened next? It was a momentous occasion for the 'wets', largely the Association Against the Prohibition Amendment (AAPA) and nothing could dampen their spirits. As the Thirties gathered pace, America was determined to celebrate its new freedom, a new freedom that would open up the way to intensified demand for the services of the cocktail shaker. These were halcyon days. Repeal was advocated with the promise of no return to the great mahogany bars of the saloon. Its successors, the bar, tavern and cocktail lounge, constitute a ubiquitous American institution. Mixing drinks at home became a ritual and to the cocktail was attributed the function of separation – the easing of the way – between work and the recreations of the evening. The quick potations of the 'cocktail hour' caught on and were assiduously imitated in many countries; the cocktail party, in full swing, pitchforked the cocktail shaker into the party whirl. The Post-Prohibition shakers, inexpensive and no longer simply the preserve of the wealthy – chrome cocktail sets on sale for $95 in 1928 were replaced with sets listed in the catalogue at $7.50 after Repeal – made a good impression among present hunters. Customers could rely with confidence on Manning Bowman's lustrous chromium-plated 'The Repealer' ('as smart and new as Repeal itself') and fitted with an Arinite (their own plastic) stopper, to add zest to the cocktail hour. Cocktail cabinets, martini pitchers, serving trays and ice buckets, functional items in modern form, became a more familiar sight in domestic interiors.

It was party time in America, the era of the big bands, big night-

Seeing red: a Napier cocktail measure with side-grip release; a ruby red glass recipe shaker with flat top; a similar example with domed top and cap; a Napier jigger and tongs, a Bell measure and bottle opener; a silver-plated measure with horizontal markings and handle. All American, 1930s.

clubs and big tabs. 'Now our Night Life Glows Anew' reported *The New York Times Magazine*, 'New York life has come out into the open. It is right back to being a public spectacle instead of a secret rite with a suggestion of brimstone and black magic about it.' In the opinion of the grand panjandrum, columnist Walter Winchell, who once referred to the speakeasy crowd as 'gintellectuals', clubs like the swanky Rainbow Room, opened in 1934, El Morocco – in an age when the *maitre d'hôtel*, not the chef, was the crowd-puller, customers broke down in frustration at 'Elmo' for failing to catch his eye – and the Stork, 'New York's New Yorkiest place', were in the ascendant. Charles Chaplin, J. Paul Getty and Alfred Vanderbilt all married

Downhill racer: a stylised skier slaloms through the marker flags and over the surface of this rare American cocktail shaker, c.1935. The design is overlaid in sterling silver and reproduced on each piece of the frosted glass set, including the six martini glasses and tray.

On the distaff side: Rose, daughter of an English landlord, shows off her skills with the cocktail shaker in a New York Hotel where she works as a bartender, 1948. Canadian research claims a classic 'shaken' martini contains more helpful antioxidant chemicals than a 'stirred' version but gives no idea why there should be a difference. Leading cocktail exponents have discovered flaws in the research.

Moscow Mule

2 parts Smirnoff vodka
½ part lime juice
4 parts ginger beer

Shake the lime juice and vodka then strain into ice-filled highball glass. Add ginger beer and garnish with lime wedge.

Invented in 1936 in the Cock'n'Bull in Los Angeles by a man who wanted to promote Smirnoff vodka, a woman who had a large number of copper mugs and a man who had lots of ginger beer; necessity is the mother of invention.

women whom they met at the Stork. One over-refreshed customer left a disbelieving waiter a $20,000 tip. Those were indeed the days.

Think of a tough act to follow as the positive epicentre of cocktail drinking, and partying in general, and there is a good chance the name Hollywood will turn up. Hollywood glamorised cocktails – the dry martini was the definitive on-screen cocktail and the 'Hollywood' a regular gin and vermouth off-screen alternative – and the cocktail shaker, against the bright backcloth of the movie colony, hit the jackpot. Cocktails were the pastime of the film crowd and their hangers-on, the literati and any assortment of minor nobility. Everyone

Vintage stuff: a c.1934 American mixer set in Art Deco style, comprising a large shaker with angular decoration and lid fittings, in sterling silver, with matching glasses, demonstrating that the cocktail shaker was capable of decorative as well as utilitarian effects.

wanted to be part of the scene. The film studios, expressing the hope of better times, tendered temporary escape from the daily round and thrilled a nation. Cinema-goers were accustomed to expect the constant availability of drama, music, sensation and fun. The leading art director Cedric Gibbons' visit to the 1925 Paris Exhibition haunted a corner of his imagination, as seen in the settings for MGM's *Our Dancing Daughters*, and the Moderne style provides the back-drop to Busby Berkeley's extravaganza *Gold Diggers of 1933*, and the highly successful musicals starring Fred Astaire and Ginger Rogers.

For the majority, the great and often the only entertainment was cinema, and many Americans were first intrigued by Moderne accoutrements on a visit to the local movie-palace, transformed into an Art Deco showpiece. The new photo magazines, supported by studio publicity, promoted the lifestyle of Hollywood aristocrats and, at home, stars attempted to recreate the lavish set designs they had left behind after a day's shooting. Scenic designs for American films in the Moderne style provided fertile ground for British architect-designers, inspiring them to dispense with period detail in their work.

Nothing could better illustrate 'Tinseltown's' love affair with cocktail culture than the prime example of *The Thin Man* series of screwball comedies based on Dashiell Hammett's detective fiction. Nick and Nora Charles, suave husband and wife sleuths, played by William Powell and Myrna Loy, appeared on the screen a year after Repeal in *The Thin Man*, the first of a series of six films extended over thirteen years starring the detective team, and nominated for an Academy Award for Best Picture of 1934. The polished and apparently light-hearted Nick is prodigiously successful at solving murders and drinking plenty of dry martinis (like Nora). His demonstration before an assemblage of bartenders on how properly to mix drinks – 'Important thing is the rhythm, always have rhythm in your shaking' – is a useful reminder to aspiring mixologists of how it should be done.

Luxury Cruises

The rhythm continued in Europe and, curiously enough, at sea, where the cocktail shaker was coming up in the world. Excursions to Norway, Spain and Portugal, Morocco, the Canaries and the Western Mediterranean were popularised through cruises. This novel form of travel was encouraged by the shipping companies at the start of the decade when the Wall Street crash cut American tourist traffic alarmingly and the owners had to do something to keep their vessels afloat.

Just the one: English silver-plated cocktail cherry-olive bowl with enamel stem and six cocktail sticks with cherry heads, 1930s, 'Just a Thimbleful' spirit measure, six silver-plated cocktail whisks and stand, two cocktail-shaker shaped Napier jiggers, a snail cocktail stick holder, French, 1930s; chrome and Bakelite ice tong and a spring-loaded cocktail measuring funnel in the Art Deco style, on an ebonised base, French, 1920s.

The trips were in demand among the English, unable to manage a Continental holiday due to sterling depreciation, but looking for a change from the English seaside. Ship's officers undertook to organise all kinds of entertainments – swimming, deck sports, fancy-dress competitions, concert and cinema shows, galas and cocktail parties. Cruises were one long party and many mothers took their daughters on board in the hope of finding suitable husbands for them. Cocktail parties represented a useful staging post in a flirtation and the shipping companies advertised their success as 'Cupid's agents'. In an age before aerial links, the ocean liner was one of the principal achievements in industrial progress and national prestige. In 1935, the French *Compagnie Générale Transatlantique* turned their attention to the launch of their luxury liner *Normandie*, the most glamorous ship in the world in the Thirties and a showcase for contemporary design. The interior decoration, for those who had the wonderful good

Unmistakably English: a silver-plated Georgian style cocktail shaker from Asprey; a 'Zeeronator' silver-plated shaker with Bakelite top; a coffee pot-style shaker with cork stopper for a spout; a Dunhill shaker with chain-affixed stopper, and a further example resembling a coffee pot; all English, 1930s.

Trompe l'Oeil: photographer R.J. Salmon prepares a cocktail for himself, 1936. The main criterion of success for a *trompe l'oeil* is its ability to deceive the eye as to the material reality of the objects represented.

fortune to travel as passengers, was commissioned from the top crafts-men of the day. The first-class restaurant, a shade larger than the Hall of Mirrors at Versailles, was a superb creation with Lalique features, hammered in bronze and glass and with superb silver tableware designed in Georg Jensen's Danish workshops. The *Normandie's* Grand Salon was portrayed as 'a room full of silver, gold, and glass, large as a theatre, floating through the ever clean, endless ocean just outside the big window'.

Few makers enjoy such a reputation as Georg Jensen. The Danish master opened his first shop in Copenhagen in 1904, and branches followed in New York, London, Paris and other European cities. Jensen produced, with Johan Rohde and Harald Neilsen, luxury silver and metal workpieces, many radical in design. In the Thirties the Jensen workshops retained the equally gifted Sigvard Bernadotte, responsible for their linear incised engraved bodies. Bernadotte's cocktail shaker sets, finished to the highest standards, and of real distinction, are considered some of the most attractive ever made.

Hans Hansen established his studio in Kolding, Denmark two years

On track: rare silver-plated cocktail set in the form of a Great War tank, comprising shaker with long spout, six shot cups, maker unknown, English 1920s.

86

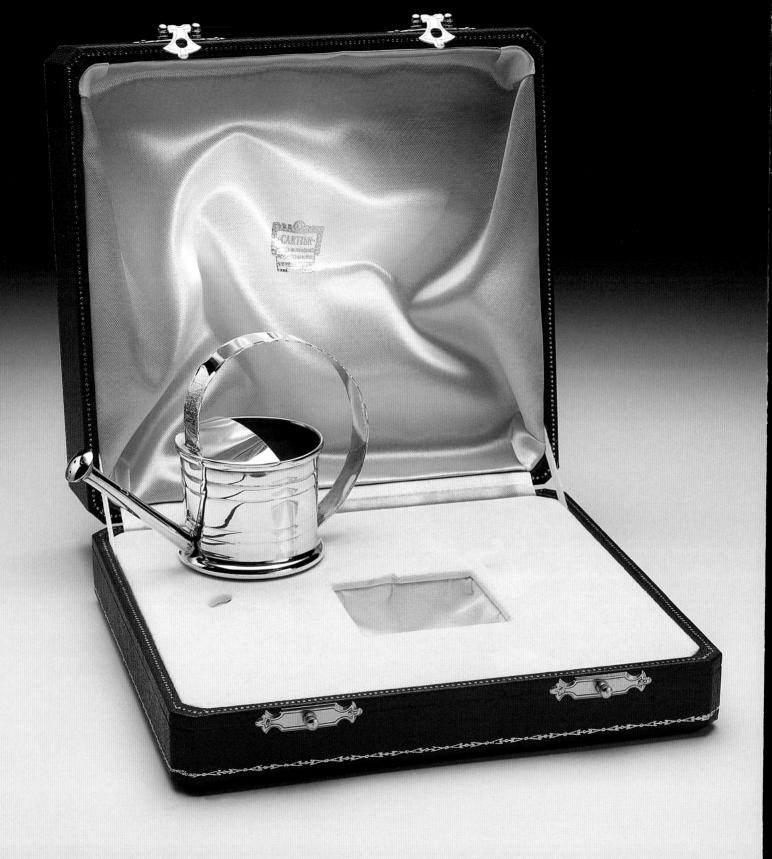

Danish style: a barman pours a cocktail in a bar in Copenhagen, 1956. Denmark's capital was a popular rallying point for cocktails in Scandinavia where designers set a consistently high standard in shaker design.

(Left) Name dropper: Cartier sterling silver vermouth dropper in the form of a watering can, 1930s.

(Right) Sterling area: a Danish silver shaker, attributed to Karl M. Cohr, Fredericia, 1944, and a Belgian silver Art Deco cocktail shaker, makers mark of Wolfers Fr., Brussels, c.1930.

The hand of the master: finished to perfection, Sigvard Bernadotte's superb 1937 cocktail set, no. 819, for Georg Jensen, represents the glories of Danish design.

Margarita

2 parts José Cuervo
tequila
1 part cointreau
1 part fresh lime juice

Shake all and strain into chilled Salud Grande glass with salted rim. Garnish with lime wheel.

Created by American socialite Margaret Sames, whilst holidaying in Acapulco. Her friendship with Nicky Hilton (of Hilton hotel fame) helped make this drink one the most popular cocktails in America.

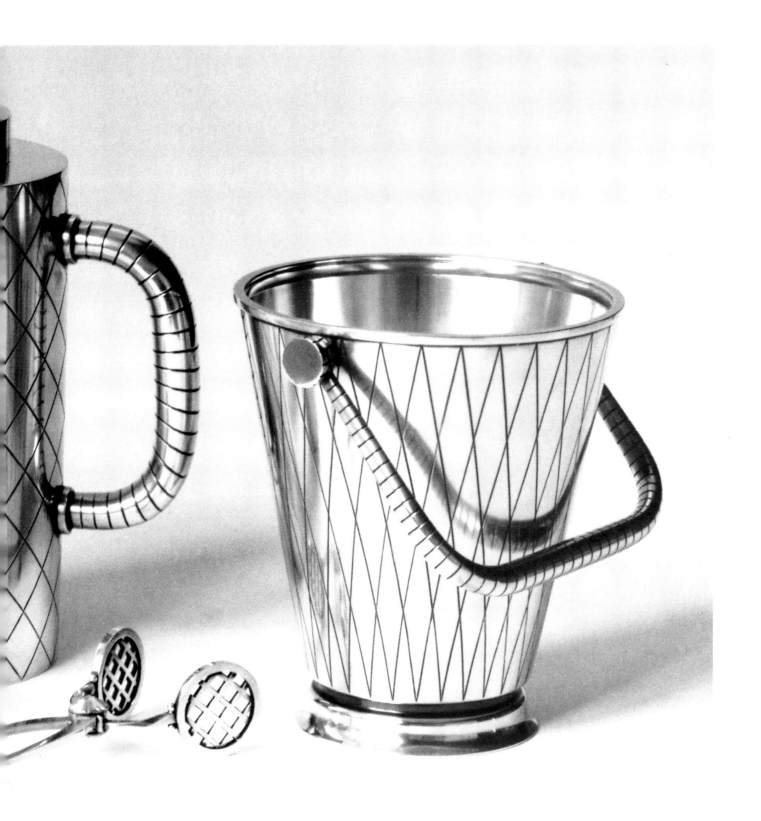

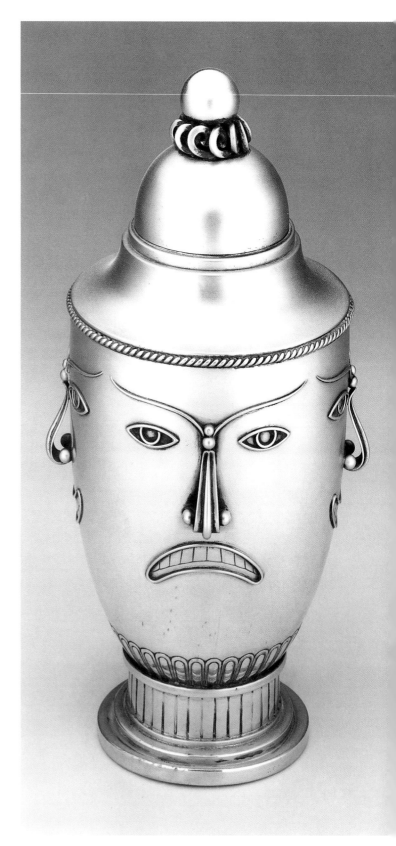

The faces of the shaker (front and back) Georg Thylstrup's highly individualistic design, executed in 1933 for the Danish firm of Grann & Laglye, arouses both interest and excitement at the Brohan-Museum in Berlin where it is on permanent display.

after his rival Jensen. Hansen's reputation was established by his use of unblemished silver surfaces and precise planning and craftsmanship in geometric form for his modern silverwares. An example of his cylindrical cocktail shaker, completed in 1934, is exhibited at the Brohan-Museum, Berlin, a fitting tribute to the accomplished maker's craft. Karl Gustave Hansen, his son, succeeded him as artistic director in 1940. The Scandinavian manufacturer Grann and Laglye stand out for their innate sense of design and are represented in the Brohan-Museum by uncompromising individuality in the shape of a pair of mask-like cocktail shakers from Georg Thylstrup, who also contributed distinctive pieces for the Danish ceramicists, Ipsens Enke. P. Koch and Bergfeld, the Bremen silver studio, are the last in our trio of cocktail shaker designers celebrated at the Berlin museum, where a highly original flagon-style shaker created in 1935 by George Elsass is displayed. Elsass had followed the sculptor Hugh Leven as head of the firm's design studio. Koch and Bergfeld attached less importance than other workshops to working with front-ranking

Thirties' style: commendable evidence of form by the New Zealand designer, Keith Murray, who was also one of the most important practitioners of engraved wares. Murray moved to England in the early Thirties and his cocktail set shown here, including eight martini goblets and tray, was completed c.1935 for Mappin & Webb, manufacturing silversmiths, established in 1863.

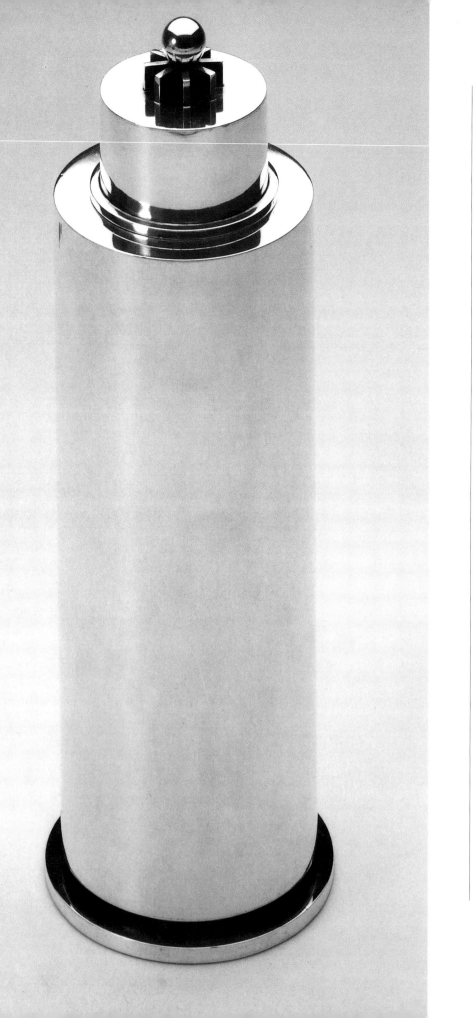

(Left) Danish silversmiths: cylindrical shaker from Hans Hansen, who established a silver studio at Kolding in 1906. Hansen produced modern silverwares in the Thirties and the precision of finish to his work cannot be overestimated. He succeeded handsomely with the design of this shaker in 1934.

(Right) Radically modern: Gustav Elsass created a pioneering and prolific body of work, including his contributions to the German silver workshop/company, Koch & Bergfeld. Here is his advanced design for a cocktail shaker for the Bremen company in the form of a flagon, made in 1935 and also on display at the Brohan Museum.

independent artists (of which Elsass was unquestionably one). The company was acquired by Villeroy and Boch in 1989.

Another driving force among designers was a former architect, a New Zealander working in London on whom the Scandinavian designers were a formative influence. Keith Murray's special territory was glass and he was one of the most important contributors to British design. He came to prominence as a designer for Stevens and Williams (later Royal Brierley Crystal) of Stourbridge, and also produced ceramics for Wedgwood. Murray's primary concern was with form and all his glass pieces, including the cocktail shakers which generate a great deal of interest, were hand-made.

In popular memory Britons are remembered as enjoying jokes about Prohibition, always representing more of an ideal than a reality, and a measure dubbed by King George V, despite his natural reserve, as an 'outrage'. Nevertheless, 'private bottle parties' were contrived in the early Thirties following the hard line taken by the licensing authorities over nightclubs towards the end of the previous decade. Nothing could shake the determination of visitors to London, or residents, to drink out of hours, or the determination of nightclub proprietors to profit from it. The theory behind bottle parties was straightforward: so long as the organisers of such a party were 'hosts', and customers 'guests', the powers that be had no right to oppose drinking, dancing, music or any other form of entertainment held at a private event. House rules at the early bottle parties were rigorous, and discretion prevailed. It was impossible to secure a drink unless the order for it had been placed hours before by the 'host', and a printed invitation was absolutely essential. Attempts to 'gate-crash' were met with a firm refusal from irreproachably behaved staff. The host's benevolence unsurprisingly stopped far short of gratuitous hospitality and, feeling obliged to ask for some little help to meet his expenses over the pleasure at welcoming so many 'friends', charged at well above the going rate for cocktails, inferior champagne and other potables. Top-line dance-bands were booked to play in these Elysian surroundings.

Soon, however, premises sprang up without pretensions either to luxury or good service, and with the Lord Chamberlain powerless to act, well-to-do roisterers (bottle parties were usually beyond the financial reach of younger society) were entertained to the semi-nude cabaret. Soho 'vice' kings, bookmakers, professional and amateur prostitutes, out of town businessmen, officers on leave and the adventurous in search of London's nightlife made up the clientele. Bottle

Martini di Arma di Taggia's Martini

2 parts TANQUERAY® gin
2 parts dry vermouth
1 dash orange bitters

Shake all and strain into chilled cocktail glass.

Another candidate for the title of creator of the martini supposedly mixed by Signor Martini for his most famous customer – John D. Rockefeller – at the Knickerbocker Hotel in New York, 1910.

'Tells-U-How' (A): many cocktail enthusiasts considered a 'Tells-U-How' Mixer set to be an essential part of life. The notably handsome two-tone, silver-plated Asprey version, whose outer sleeves turned to reveal recipes for sixteen different cocktails, was launched in the Thirties and is considered in a class by itself – every collection should have one.

parties rarely opened before midnight and, as the last 'guests' were helped into waiting taxi-cabs, rarely shut before six or seven in the morning. At one time, fifty-two clubs – exotic names were customary and the Old Florida, the Coconut Grove, the Blue Lagoon and the Havana were among the best known ones – were counted in the vicinity of five West End streets. A crackdown was inevitable, and in May 1939, numbers were halved, the cabaret girls given notice and drinks prices reduced to the level of the Embassy Club, a favourite haunt of Edward, Prince of Wales.

In January 1936, eight months after his 25th Jubilee, King George V was laid to rest with his ancestors in the chapel of Windsor Castle. His eldest son, who had spent much of the Twenties touring the globe, and who had expressed his liking for the informality of the manners of the American rich, succeeded him as Edward VIII. The

'Tells-U-How' (B): a sample of 'Tells-U-How' cocktail shakers from England, America and Italy, 1930s, and a later chrome-finished model, demonstrating the lasting popularity of the design. During the Thirties in Italy, much industrial design was produced by small workshop manufacturers.

Pass the ice: cold storage facilities from makers such as Christofle, Elkington, Cartier and Tiffany, 1930s. Ice machines and cubed ice are relatively recent inventions in the story of the shaker. 'Trader' Vic described ice as 'the first requisite of good mixing' and a warm cocktail as 'revolting'.

fixed interests of the new monarch were foxhunting and steeplechasing, golf and clothes – he popularised many unconventional modes of dress – and metropolitan nightclubs. It was alleged he kept raffish company and was impatient of dull functions. The song, 'I danced with a man who danced with a girl who danced with the Prince of Wales', suited the mood of the times and was testament to the fascination the bachelor Prince held for many of the nation.

As the year drew to its close, the King made clear his wishes to take legislative steps which would permit him to marry a commoner, Mrs Simpson, a twice-divorced American occasionally mentioned in Court Circulars, but without making her his Queen. A single change of heart might have been condoned in the Thirties but not more. The British Cabinet met in November under Prime Minister Stanley Baldwin and unanimously decided that such action was unconstitutional. It could not have been foreseen what would happen. Newspapers were filled with the 'Grave Constitutional Crisis' and the *Times* urged the King to make up his mind. Mrs Simpson went to

Against all convention: the marriage in France of the former King Edward VIII and Wallis Simpson, 3 June 1937, decently featured in the popular press, though virtually ignored by the broadsheets. Official new sources continued to divert public attention from the Duke and Duchess following their marriage.

France and was said to have pleaded with the King not to give up his throne on her behalf. Edward VIII Coronation mugs sold out. The suspense continued until 3 December 1936 when Baldwin read the royal message of Abdication to a hushed Parliament. On the same evening, the King, now Duke of Windsor, broadcast his farewell speech to the nation. His brother, George VI, succeeded to the throne and was crowned in May 1937. The Duke of Windsor married Mrs Simpson in a quiet ceremony at Candé, France on 3 June in the same

The Windsor shaker: a glass cocktail shaker with chrome top, engraved 'June 3rd 1937' to commemorate the wedding day of the Duke and Duchess of Windsor.

SOTHEBY'S

562

The Duke & Duchess of Windsor

September 11–19, 1997

year. The wedding was decently featured in the popular press and, significantly, among the many presents was a glass cocktail shaker, fitted with a chrome top, and engraved 'June 3rd 1937', a gift from the members of the couple's Paris household.

In a sense George Berry's Golf Bag cocktail set from the Twenties wrote the job description for every subsequent novelty cocktail shaker. The shaker, once only for the few, was now owned by a great many families and sales had tailed off. The manufacturers, impressed with the commercial possibilities presented by novelty versions, and seeking to engage the interest of a wider public, rose to the occasion by dreaming up a multitude of new designs in an attempt to outdo one another. No matter how wacky the designs – much energy had

'W.W.': the Duchess of Windsor's personal travelling cocktail set, comprising a silver cocktail shaker, two flasks, two cups and a spoon, housed in a leather carrying case. All engraved 'W.W.' for Wallis Windsor. Edward VIII's pursuit of Wallis Simpson cost him his crown.

Work in Progress: barman at the Embassy Club in London, 1933. The Embassy was a favourite of the bachelor Prince of Wales. His Abdication filled a great number of newspaper columns but the nightclub lost much of its popularity following his exile.

gone into dumb-bells, dinner bells, bowling pins and even a lady's legs – the novelty cocktail shaker was always usable. Their appeal was to the eye and zealous supporters of the new shapes described them as 'amusing' – this adjective had succeeded the Victorian 'chic' and the Edwardian 'smart' as a term of praise for any notably eccentric novelty during the Thirties. The new arrivals provided the excuse for an invitation, and many cocktail parties were enlivened by their appearance, but for the most part they did not catch on widely. Today, however, the makers' best achievements conjure up an epoch and are cherished by the astute collector.

By a common verdict, the most generally beloved of novelty shakers is the Penguin, designed by E. A. Schuelke and manufactured by Napier of Meriden. The costume jewellery makers, named after its

Pin up: chrome and maplewood bowling pin set, American, c.1935. Novelty cocktail shakers, anticipated by George Berry's golf-bag design and part of the colourful history of the shaker, were decorative, practical and fun.

president James H. Napier, and founded in 1922, applied for a drink mixer patent ten years later. The Napier 'Foursome', a quartet of smaller cocktails shakers in a Tantalus frame (a stand with a grooved bar to keep the shakers in place), appeared for 1934. A dial indicator was affixed to the top of each individual shaker in this inventive set, to eliminate the chance of anyone getting the wrong drink as all four cocktails were shaken at the same time. The Cone cocktail shaker made its debut in the same year and, with its non-removable strainer, could be used as a mixer for those drinks that respond better to stirring. As rival companies strove to serve the appetite of the

Enterprise of England: the premier English company Asprey made a principal contribution to cocktail shaker design at the upper end of the market and their attractive silver-plated 'Dumb-Bell' shakers from the Thirties, pictured here, were especially popular in Paris. Considered essential by collectors today.

ASPREY
LONDON
3138
MADE IN ENGLAND
PAT. APPLIED FOR 28610/35

(Left) Quartet: Napier of Meriden devised the costly Foursome cocktail shaker for 1934. The individual shakers were equipped with a dial indicator set to the chosen drink to eliminate the chance of missing the right drink. The handle of the Tantalus frame is clamped down and all four shakers may be shaken at once.

(Right) Family likeness: a large and small beer barrel cocktail shaker from the Thirties, and a 'Dimple' Haig whiskey shaker with distinctive 'pinch' bottle, introduced in 1929 by the International Silver Company, following the success of the Golf Bag and Lighthouse cocktail shaker versions.

consumer, Napier played their hand superbly by introducing Emil Schuelke's Penguin for the 1936 Christmas season. The endearing silver-plated figure with opening beak to reveal rubber stopper and pourer was also finished in chromium, but usually on sale without a manufacturer's mark. It is not recorded whether Napier produced, or authorised, the modification.

Many continue to believe, not without justification, that Norman Bel Geddes, listed by *Forbes* magazine in 1936 as one of the top five American industrial designers, was the principal star in the firmament in an age which showed such faith in design; an age brought to a close by the advent of war. Norman Bel Geddes worked briefly as an advertising draughtsman before moving on to the theatre, supported by international banker Otto Kahn, champion of Ritz and Escoffier. Bel Geddes designed, and produced and directed, plays and went on to Hollywood to design sets for Cecil B. de Mille and D.W. Griffith. He was influenced by the German Expressionist architect, Erich Mendelsohn and, in 1924, Mendelsohn gave him a book of his designs and a rendering of his Einstein tower, an early example of streamlining. Three years later, Bel Geddes opened the first industrial design studio in America to encourage the concepts of design and styling

Bowled over: a group of bowling-related pieces including a rare skittle set produced in 1937 by Dunhill. A shrinking market gave rise to the novelty cocktail shaker and manufacturers deliberately attempted designs of considerable originality in an effort to find new customers.

All the rage: Emil Schuelke's imaginatively conjured silver-plated Penguin cocktail shaker, the beak opens to reveal a rubber stopper and pourer, introduced by Napier in 1936. The costume jewellery firm produced a line of silver-plated gifts during the Thirties including Schuelke's design. The genial penguin, beloved symbol of the best of all periods for the cocktail shaker, is one to thrill the hearts of collectors. Beware imitations.

which heralded the new technological age. The leading propagandist for streamlining, he was the first to gain public recognition as a consultant designer when a profile of him appeared in a 1930 issue of *Fortune* magazine and, in 1932, his technologically orientated outlook was captured in his book, *Horizons*, in which he defined the designer's role and methods. One of the few to employ consumer surveys, Bel Geddes scrutinised competitor's products, and analysed the design objective – the product's intended function, and the way it was made, sold and serviced – along with the manufacturer's own capacity.

He was appointed to the planning board of the 1933 Chicago Fair and the New York World's Fair, 1939, creating for General Motors,

Bordello red: the timeless appeal of a 'Thirst Extinguisher' cocktail shaker, English, c.1930; a skyscraper, and the favourite of many, a lady's leg shaker by West Virginia Specialty Glass c.1937 with chrome top and removable high heel (both attributed to the Derby Shelton Silver Co.). The survival rate of the fanciful lady's leg shaker is low.

Joy Producers: a series of bell-shaped cocktail shakers including a silver-plated 'Joy Bell' from Birmingham silversmiths Hukin & Heath, for Asprey, c.1935; another English handbell with stepped decoration and wooden handle, a chrome bellshaker with glasses, American 1930s, and a further example of an English bell shaker, 1930s.

The 'Pondering God' Martini

4 parts TANQUERAY® gin
1 part chablis
rinse of kirsch
olive stuffed with truffles

Shake gin and wine. Rinse glass with kirsch. Garnish with olive.

Invented by P.G. Wodehouse at the Aerobleu. One tester started off proclaiming 'Mon Dieu' in admiration, then 'Mon Dieu' in stupefaction, then started to have visions, hence the name.

who towered over the American automobile industry in the Thirties, a markedly futuristic pavilion at Long Island, attracting a record ten million visitors. His work in standardisation for home furnishing equipment was pioneering, and the Rome Manufacturing Company, a division of Revere Copper and Brass Incorporated, considered the visionary designer's work 'caught skilfully the tempo of our times', and retained his services from 1934. The giftware line for the following year's catalogue was designed primarily by Bel Geddes and, in 1936, his justly famous Manhattan skyscraper cocktail shaker set was released – a consummate streamlined design in polished chromium, moderated by an assurance of intelligence and good taste. The Revere 'Cocktail Ensemble', complete with a Bel Geddes-designed stepped tray, was trumpeted by its makers as offering a 'practical as well as decorative note'. (It seems almost an infallible rule with cocktail shakers that what looks right is right). One of the most celebrated creations in cocktail shaker history, collectors line up for this one.

Revere, named to perpetuate Paul Revere, the silversmith and copperplate printer who was one of the party that destroyed the tea in Boston Harbour in 1773, put themselves firmly on the cocktail shaker map with the 'Manhattan' and, in 1938, excelled themselves by issuing two exceptional shakers from a native of Scotland, their

Frivolity rules: a ruby glass cocktail shaker decorated with hunting motif, a dumbell shaker and American 'curly wurly', c.1930. Check the attic for Novelty shakers – although sales, despite great ingenuity by the makers, were modest rather than reasonable, the Thirties' shakers have captured the imagination of present-day collectors.

The Big One: the streamlined cocktail shaker by Norman Bel Geddes, the godfather of industrial design, produced for Revere in 1936. The chromium-plated shaker stands out as one of the finest designs ever realised and retains a legendary status among serious collectors. The complete 'Ferris Wheel' ensemble is extremely rare.

Director of Design, William Archibald Welden. The first design credits of W. Archibald Welden, ex-consultant designer to Revere who developed a diversified metalware product line in close association with its technicians, appeared in the 1937 giftware catalogue. Customers for Welden's chrome-plated brass Empire and Zephyr cocktail shakers of the following season, unmistakably of their time, were invited to consider seven different serving sets, including the Ascot, Park and Sheridan. Examples which survive, through freakish good fortune, or the careful prescience of the owner, can look stunning in a contemporary setting.

As far as Britain was concerned, there were signs in the late Thirties of a move towards a more conventional approach to drinking. Cocktails were by no means extinguished but the gin-and-tonic mix had replaced some of the more formidable compounds and the cocktail party was eclipsed by the sensible sherry party. Serious commentators sensed the coming conflict and *The Spectator* reported ' a week whose first four days have been marked by no accentuation of crisis is by common consent being described as a period of "lull" in international affairs'. The newspapers of 1939 still carried lists of wedding presents (cocktail shaker sets included) and the smart set sunned themselves – Eden Roc, Biarritz and Le Touquet were full to the brim – as the exchange of diplomatic notes continued. The Paris Collections of August 1939 were more frivolous, lavish and extreme than for years but, by the end of the month, the fall of the curtain for the cocktail age in Europe was very close. Spirits were placed on quota during the Second World War, excise taxes doubled and only a small fraction of pre-war sales allocated to the wholesale and retail trade. Gin was never officially rationed – the 'allowance', if you could ever find it, was reckoned to equal about a bottle a month. A black market sprang up, and the distribution of dubiously obtained gin, often counterfeit, was a reminder of the Prohibition years in America. As the resolve of the country was tested to the full, bars managed to stay open, although for many of their customers social life disappeared altogether.

The 1940 October issue of *Architectural Forum* in America was devoted exclusively to the decade just closed, especially the achievements in 'relating machine inspired design to a machine inspired way of life'. The journal noted: 'With the emergence of the designer as the conscious exponent of a machine aesthetic, design enters a new stage. Not only are the arts influenced by the machine, but the reverse is also now true. It is this interplay of influences that give the 1930–40 period – the 'Design Decade' – its peculiar interest and importance.'

In the same year, the Director of the San Francisco Museum of Art, Grace McCann Morley, encapsulated the attainments of the 'Design Decade': 'The last ten years have seen a tremendous development in arts, crafts, and industrial design in this country. Influences from abroad, discoveries in techniques and new materials, the creativeness of young designers aware of contemporary living in the United States, growing penetration of art into industry, combined to make this a period worth noting in the evolution of contemporary styles. Modern design techniques that were at first superficial and purely decorative have settled into a sincere harmony between form and function, and standards of both execution and of appreciation have noticeably risen. In many fields, a distinctive contemporary style has emerged.' It was a not unperceptive analysis that the design avant garde in America, largely centred on New York, had exhibited courage of conviction in their indigenous style and ultimately surpassed Paris as style leader.

Novel ideas: milk churn cocktail shakers including the rare Asprey model, c.1935, not listed in the main catalogue, and examples from Tiffany in America, Shreve Crump & Low and two other, unknown, English makers – all dating from the Thirties, heyday of the cocktail shaker.

Kromekraft: a Farber Brothers chrome, ribbed-design cocktail shaker by Kromekraft (their trademark) with Bakelite trim, American, 1930s; a similarly finished, jug-shaped shaker, marked L.B., American, c.1935, and the extremely accomplished 'Empire' cocktail shaker, in chromium and Bakelite, by W. Archibald Welden for Revere, a design of great merit. Another Kromekraft shaker from the same decade completes the line-up.

President Roosevelt modified America's neutrality in favour of the Allies and many distillers, including the hyper-patriotic Lewis Rosensteil, head of Schenley's, turned to making industrial alcohol for the war effort. Roosevelt met economic crisis with his 'New Deal' but saw the Depression reach its close as his country was brought into the struggle following the bombing of the base at Pearl Harbour in December 1941. Cocktail shaker production was halted as the manufacturers retooled for war-related work, and prepared to play an active role in defence production. Thermos, who had offered cocktail shakers in their range since 1935, were given the highest civilian priority to continue the manufacture of vacuum bottles as all giftware

Infinite variety: pail-shaped jigger from Cartier; a Napier measure and spoon; a Cartier vermouth dropper; a cocktail shaker, engraved EVG; a Gorham stoplight jigger; a Napier musical measure, a sterling silver salt and pepper set in the form of miniature cocktail shakers, and a sterling silver Tiffany 'Oil Can' vermouth dropper.

Counter attack: Lucy Clayton, later to open a highly successful modelling agency and 'charm' school, learns the basic elements of mixing drinks at the 1936 Wines, Spirits and Hotel Trades Fair held in London.

(Left) Prestigious: a spectacular and very rare sterling silver cocktail shaker set, incorporating six goblets and tray, with matching gadroon edge detail, by Wolfers, c.1930s. The foremost Belgian jewellers, located in Brussels, employed gifted contemporary designers, gaining much well-deserved prestige for their creations, and ranked alongside French rivals, Cartier, Lalique and Puiforcat.

(Right) Jingle bells: novelty time in the shape of a silver-plated baby's rattle with wooden handle, American, c.1930s. By the early Thirties in London, a new phenomenon, 'ladies who lunch', had appeared, and generally, modish merrymaking was enlivened by beverages of the 'this cocktail is so strong, I'm not sure I should be drinking this' school. (They did anyway.)

Mayfair chic: cocktail drinking in Mayfair as seen by *Picture Post* magazine, 1939. By the late Thirties in London, the cocktail party had given way to the sherry party but cocktail bars were still a first choice rendezvous for 'ladies who lunch'.

Prairie Oyster

2 dashes vinegar
1 egg yolk
1 teaspoonful Worcester sauce
1 teaspoonful tomato catsup
1 dash pepper on top

Do not break the egg yolk.

The definitive hangover cure, compounded by Eddie Clark, bartender at The Savoy during the Second World War.

Vacuum-packed: a smart Italian cocktail shaker set with the tall shaker complemented by six Manhattan glasses, six cocktail glasses and a tray, and a vellum covered Thermos jug, 1940s. Thermos, the trademark of the American Bottle Company, produced cocktail shakers, and thermal ice buckets, from 1935.

production ceased. Manning Bowman, receiving a contract to produce 'Venturi' spun metal tubes for attachment to glider wings, experienced difficulties in obtaining the raw materials specified for the order. 'Venturi' tubes had to be capable of withstanding extreme pressures for five minutes on the flaring side of the tubes and then springing back into their original shape. The plant superintendent at Manning Bowman, pressed by Air Technical Service Command for delivery of the tubes, remembered that there were 3,000 brass cases remaining from their Grenadier cocktail shakers in store, unfinished when consumer production was stopped to conserve chromium.

All sorts of everything: a sterling silver Aztec engraved cocktail shaker, Mexican, c.1940; a sterling silver shaker from Tiffany, American, 1930s; a German silver shaker and cup, 1930s, and an example of the Mexican-made 'Silver Bullet', 1930s.

'The Rapid': a silver-plated champagne cork-style pepper mill by Peugeot, long established as a prosperous metalworking firm before turning to cars, 1920s; a Bellhop salt and pepper shaker; 'The Rapid', an innovative bevelled glass cocktail shaker operated by a plunger on the lid – when the plunger is depressed, the attached 'paddles' mix the drink – English, late 1930s; a swizzle stick holder and six sticks, English, 1930s, and a Napier silver-plated measure with side grip to release into the glass, 1930s.

Pegu

1 ½ parts TANQUERAY® gin
½ part cointreau
½ part lime juice
2 dashes angostura bitters

Shake all and strain into
chilled cocktail glass.
Garnish with lime twist.

*The house cocktail of the
Pegu Club in Rangoon.
One of the most sought-
after drinks of the
Twenties and Thirties,
much missed today.*

Manning Bowman modified the tubes to meet the contract specifications and the 'Grenadier' went to war. 'We feel that very probably our cocktail shaker was the only one to take part in the European invasion' said a Manning Bowman spokesman, 'certainly the only one to serve as a glider part. Before the war, we marketed this particular shaker under the name 'Grenadier'. After the war when we start peacetime production again, we may call it the "Invader".' History has a tendency to defy orderly classification and Manning Bowman, in company with a number of its former rivals, never returned to shaker production. It is pleasant to record that by no means had the last been heard of the cocktail shaker.

Machine age: a silver-plated cocktail shaker, machine-turned, with removable strainer, English, 1930s; a glass shaker overlaid in silver with comical drinking scenes, American, 1930s; a clear glass shaker from that period, and decorated with hunting theme, and a glass and silver-plated measure containing eight stylised Airedale swizzle sticks.

BOND AND BEYOND

'The renaissance of the hotel bar owes a lot to the revival of cocktail bar culture and the rediscovery of the classic martini'

FINANCIAL TIMES, NOVEMBER 1999

It is history that scarcity remained the lot of all in the early Fifties. New clothes were luxuries and foreign holidays unaffordable. Nevertheless, enthusiasm was not dampened and the young, particularly, excited by the vitality of American popular music, perceived better times ahead. The worldwide pattern of total alcohol consumption on a per capita basis increased generally and in the United States a building boom saw the growth of single family homes multiply in the decade more than at any other time. The construction of bars in basements, or 'rec' rooms, as Americans set up new homes suggests an explanation for the brief renewal of interest in the traditional cocktail shaker. 'Do Women Really Want Outside Jobs?' asked *Woman's Home Companion*. Over fifty per cent of American women decided they wanted to stay at home, and the rest showed an interest in part-time occupations; the question of full-time employment was not even considered. Television was the single most important form of mass entertainment, attracting enormous audiences, and 'TV' came to dominate after supper hours. 'Labour-saving' devices in cooking, cleaning and laundering, refrigerators, tinned and bottled fruit and, the shape of things to come in cocktail preparation, 'redi-mix' drinks, all these were offered and taken up readily.

As the cocktail parties started up again, the cocktail shaker met a new adversary – the electric blender. At the flick of a switch, a regular domestic blender, an American invention, could mix most of the drinks which called for shaking with ice cubes; thicker juices and

Stepping out: hotel bars became part of fashionable life and for the great 'chef de cuisine' Escoffier allowed the opportunity of 'observing and being observed, since they are eminently adapted to the exhibiting of magnificent dresses'. It is no surprise that the inventor of 'Peche Melba' and 'tournedos Rossini' spotted that his smart customers 'only had eyes for one another'.

Bottoms Up: Fifties American cocktail sets with transfer-printed designs of polar bears, roosters (a dominant motif in cocktail culture) and pink elephants. The essence of humour is notoriously elusive but it was fashionable to manufacture items such as 'Bottoms Up' swizzle sticks, the Milkyway rocket swirl mixer and the 'Chuck-A-Luck' dice game and cocktail dispenser in the 'Fun' Fifties.

Mai Tai

2 parts golden rum
$\frac{1}{2}$ part orange curaçao
$\frac{1}{2}$ part sugar syrup
$\frac{1}{2}$ part orgeat syrup
1 part fresh lime juice

Shake all and strain into ice-filled hurricane glass. Garnish with a lime wheel.

Attributed to the pre-eminent bartender Victor Bergeron, aka 'Trader' Vic.

Bondage: James Bond (Pierce Brosnan) being briefed by 'M' (Judi Dench) in 'The World is Not Enough'.

fruit, could be added to alcohol and drinks gradually became longer. Blenders, along with battery-powered stirring devices, superseded the skill and showmanship of hand-mixing. The last word on this brief summary of the electric blender, however, belongs to the immortal 'Trader' Vic, creator of the Pacific Island theme bar: 'The use of electric drink mixers is varied and, in many cases, abused. I think that most cocktails are best stirred or shaken by hand. Putting them in an electric drink mixer often dilutes them to a sickly mess.'

The trend in Fifties-style entertaining was towards 'good cheer' and informality. Women's magazines in America advised readers to 'banish all ostentatious show from their hostessing' (although failing to provide an adequate number of little tables for your guests at a cocktail buffet was considered a blunder). Hostessing responsibilities included not only the cocktail 'hour' but the spontaneous entertaining of unannounced visitors. The illusion of spontaneity, in the name of informality, was an essential part of modern 'gracious living'.

In New York, Manhattan saw the rise of the cabaret, and a new and more intimate kind of nightspot, with clientele learning again the sensation of cocktail drinking as a natural state of being. The venerated Rainbow Room, its elegance and glamour undiminished across the gulf of time, achieved almost legendary status. First class hotels revealed their ability to produce diamond clear dry martini cocktails impeccably, and the high jinks and drinking sprees of stars like Dean Martin, Peter Lawford and other members of the Sinatra-led 'Rat Pack', downing 'See Throughs' and 'Silver Bullets' in the approved style, relieved a shaker under siege from the push-button age. 'Martinis should never be shaken' exclaimed Somerset Maugham, 'they should always be stirred so that the molecules lie sensuously on top of each other.' James Bond would disagree. What is 007 without his trademark 'shaken not stirred' martini? Ian Fleming, his creator, who insisted cocktails should be 'properly aerated', was a newspaperman before writing his thrillers on a gold-plated typewriter. The racy adventures, and unflappable grace and good manners of his protagonist – each short chapter of the books is filled with excitement and the rich detail that has been described as the Fleming sweep – combined to make James Bond the most popular secret agent in the history of spy fiction. First edition book values of *Casino Royale*, published in 1952, (a year after the debut of the vodka martini recipe) would leave even Bond both shaken and stirred.

The art of conviviality was not disturbed by the cultural revolution of the Sixties, a time of irreverence for established ideas and cocktail

Cocktails keep life from getting boring: amber glass mixer set with sterling decoration, Belgium, c.1932; map of America cocktail shaker and glasses, American 1950s; an 'Hourglass' shaker, American, late 1930s, and a humorous black and white print design, including recipes, American, 1930s.

drinking enjoyed a surprising durability. Interest in unusual bar gadgets, for imbibers in pursuit of the elusive perfect martini, was noticeable and 'the classic of classics' was at its zenith in the United States by the end of the decade. A notable foretaste of the future for the cocktail shaker appeared in 1973 in *Esquire*, who had listed the three-to-one martini (the driest the dry martini would get in the Thirties) as one of the 'Ten Best' cocktails for 1934. The magazine claimed that, 'Young people do not like martinis and they're not drinking them. Ever! Anywhere!' Anti-martini sentiments flared up in 1976, when Presidential candidate Jimmy Carter signalled his intention to abolish what he called the '$50 Martini Lunch', as part of a tax reform plan. Forbes stated that the White House denied using the expression 'The Three Martini Lunch', proving that the urge to quote is nicely matched by the tendency to misquote. One die-hard sagely observed that 'It is no longer the fashion to enjoy a three-martini lunch, or ever to enjoy lunch at all.' Two years later, a New York columnist expressed his fears for the extinction of the martini.

It might be regarded as a matter for satisfaction that both the martini cocktail, and its long-term running-mate, the cocktail shaker, from the most thrilling yesterdays, confounded expectations and have now regained their former celebrity. Hotel bars are back in vogue, as the fashion crowd seek out a more civilised drinking experience. There is a definite move back to the notion of solicitous service and matchless surroundings, provided by the grand old hotel bar where professional bartenders are the equals of their famous predecessors in skilfully mixing drinks. One more thing – the cocktail shaker has the inestimable virtue of being highly practical. In an unspoken way, no one with the history of what has gone before in mind could fail to see the promise that a new epoch for the shaker has begun. Time will tell.

Opal Martini

2 parts TANQUERAY® gin
1 part cointreau
2 parts fresh orange juice

Shake all ingredients and strain into chilled cocktail glass. Garnish with flamed orange zest.

(Above) Cutting it: cocktails for the privileged in this Parisian memoir makes a passion for fashion seem like fun.

(Right) 'Cocktail Still Life', Anon, c.1935: This evocative oil painting was possibly an advertising project.

(Left) Best of the breed: finely conceived and executed designs of infinite variety capture the spirit of the golden age of the cocktail shaker and add the finishing touch to this **Tanqueray**® Guide.

THE COCKTAIL SHAKER: THE ICEMAN COMETH

by Angus Winchester
Being a dissertation on the tripartite relationship
of mixologist, drink and shaker; musings on the
seriousness and frivolity of cocktails themselves;
basic tips for the novice iceman

An ideal cocktail should appeal to four of the five senses. The quality of the ingredients – both spirituous and non – should ensure that these lively liquids dance delicately on the tongue and the stomach whilst intriguing and stimulating the nose. The glass that holds them should be clean, chilled and of the best quality and designed to add a pleasing sensation to the hand and encourage regular sipping. Finally, it should engage the eye and inspire either reverie and introspection, or boisterous celebration. But it is the other two elements of the triptych of the ideal cocktail – barman and shaker – that provide the completed fifth element. The sound of ice tinkling seductively in a well-handled shaker is as enticing and welcoming a sound as champagne corks popping, or fine crystal tapping together in toasts: Welcome to the Cocktail Nation!

The Nineties have seen the revival of the cocktail, but not the overly sweet and childishly named *frou frou* concoctions of the Seventies fern bars, or Eighties American theme bar pastiches. The drinkers who chugged their way through massive quantities of Amaretto Sours, or Pina Coladas, are being mercifully replaced by urban *gourmands* and Bright Young Things calling for martinis, Manhattans and famous liquid classics from odd spots round the world. Both in response to, and reaction against, the Spritzer-drinking fascism of the Neo-Puritans, people are drinking less, but drinking better. Bars

Singapore Gin Sling

2 parts TANQUERAY® gin
1 part cherry brandy
1 part lemon juice
½ part sugar syrup
fill with soda

Shake all except soda. Strain into ice-filled highball glass. Top with soda and garnish with a lemon wheel.

Classic Colonial drink. Add one measure of Benedictine to make Raffles Hotel signature drink.

Fifties variety: colourful transfer-printed cocktail shakers with recipes. It was an age when the electric mixer, battery operated cocktail blender and 'redi-mix' drinks were in the ascendant. The Outboard Bar Mixer was affixed to your glass for best results and the 'Yo Yo Cocktail Mixer' was readily commended for 'playful bartenders'.

throughout the world (and a few living rooms, too) are changing from vulgar Bacchanalian dives to oases of style, sophistication and escapism. People now glide up to the bar and call for a Pegu, a martini, or a Mai Tai, and are momentarily transported to a spreading world of enchantment; a world of soft lights, seductive scents, silken music, adroit entertainment, smoke and laughter, of perfection of food and service, of wines of the finest quality, all in a setting of gold and silver brocade, velvet, iron, glass and exotic woods.

As skilled and talented as the alchemists behind the bar may be – transmogrifying the contents of dusty bottles into dulcified froth with the shaker as touchstone – their art is not unteachable. Anyone who appreciates drinking cocktails will find their pleasure enhanced by their ability to make their own; and the sense of self-satisfaction on filling up a friend's or guest's glass at home should be savoured like a well-made Sazerac.

First, always ensure a large supply of fresh ice. Ice, the mixologist's second best friend after the shaker, is used not only to chill and mix properly but also to chill the glasses themselves. Secondly, consider the cocktail shaker itself: from a purely functional viewpoint, the shaker should be made of silver, stainless steel, or glass and possess a well-fitting lid – the appearance of a damp patch on the mixer's

In pursuit: a glass cocktail shaker decorated with a hunting motif, along with various hunting glasses, English, 1940s, and a hunting cocktail set with black, white, red and green transfer-printed designs, with matching glasses, American, 1950s.

Playtime in Vegas: a Flamingo cocktail stick holder, a set of Playboy bar tools, 'Hot Member' cocktail stick holder, 'Females' by Cole, a set of saucy cocktail napkins featuring Playboy cartoons, 1956, a 'Milord' shaker-decanter with top hat and liquor pump, two Bakelite dice, corkscrew and bottle opener, Roulette cocktail glass, sterling silver dice cocktail sticks in a silver bucket and a silver-plated trident olive fork.

Mad Max Martini

4 parts TANQUERAY® gin
dash grapefruit juice

Splash juice into glass then
pour in chilled gin. Stir
with finger.

*Invented by Max Morgan,
former fighter pilot and
owner of Aerobleu in
Paris. He contrived the
'Mad Max' to quell a
rapidly developing riot in
his bar. He threw open
the doors, mixed one of
these compounds and
announced that the next
round of martinis were on
the house.*

Finalists: model Jean Dawney
with finalists at the Hyde Park
Hotel who made versions of 'The
SAS Polar Short Cut' cocktail to
celebrate the inauguration of the
SAS air service to Tokyo via the
North Pole in 1957. The first
international cocktail competition, held in 1930, was won by a
barman across the street at the
Berkeley Hotel.

shoulder is as unwelcome as drool on a pillow. But, cocktail shakers are more than just functional and if a drink tastes exquisite from a basic model, how much better will it taste if one uses one from the roll-call of shakers featured in this book?

Initially, when making drinks, add the cheapest ingredients first, and ensure the juices are always fresh and the mixers always effervescent. Read all the recipes and method fully before starting and always clean your equipment regularly and thoroughly. When measuring, be consistent; whether you use a standard legal measure, the top of a shaker, or a demijohn, make the proportions constant and good drinks will result.

As cocktail making has been compared to ballroom dancing, practice is paramount; from initial clumsy shufflings you will, with dedication, soon be gliding as effortlessly as Fred and Ginger, and hopefully you will be creative and inspired enough to invent a cocktail worthy of their names. Dear reader, armed with Simon's book and inspired by the beauty of his cocktail shakers, go forth, fill your shaker with ice, reach for that **Tanqueray®** gin bottle, and guide others to the Cocktail Nation!

Picture Credits

Pullman Gallery
front cover, back cover, pp. 2, 3, 5 (bottom right), 13, 14, 17, 18, 22, 25, 29, 30, 32, 34, 35, 36, 37, 38, 39 (right), 40, 42, 43, 44, 45, 48, 49, 50, 51, 52, 53, 54, 58, 60 (bottom), 61, 62, 63, 64, 65, 66, 68, 70, 71, 72, 73, 74, 75, 76, 77, 79, 80, 82, 84, 85, 87, 88, 89 (bottom), 93, 97, 98, 99, 101, 102, 104, 105, 106, 107, 108, 109, 110, 111, 112, 113, 114–15, 116–17, 118, 120, 121, 123, 124, 125, 126, 130–31, 134, 136, 137 (bottom), 139, 140

Hulton Getty Picture Gallery
pp. 9, 12, 15, 23, 27, 39 (left), 46, 57, 59, 60 (top right), 67, 81, 86, 89 (top), 100, 103, 119, 122, 141

Mary Evans Picture Library
pp. 5 (bottom left), 10, 20, 128, 137 (top)

Brohan-Museum, Berlin
pp. 92, 94, 95

Eon Productions
p. 132

Royal Copenhagen
pp. 90–91

Cocktail Recipes

Index

Numbers in bold refer to illustrations.